The Economics Manual: Skills at A and AS level

Richard Welford.

The Author:

Richard Welford was educated at Coventry Polytechnic, Trent Polytechnic and Leicester University. He is currently a lecturer in Economics at Portsmouth Polytechnic. Previously, he was Head of Economics and Business Studies at Swanwick Hall School, Derbyshire. He is an examiner in A level Economics and a chief examiner for Information Technology. He has had a number of articles published on Economics, Computing and Education.

Editors:

Bren Abercrombie, Mary Ayres and Janet Day.

Acknowledgements:

Thanks are due to all those people who have encouraged me in the writing of this book and in particular to Jonathan Wilson for helpful comments on final drafts of the book. I am also indebted to my past and present students.

I also wish to thank the London University Examination Board for permission to use quotations from their Examiners' Reports and *The Economist* for permission to reproduce copyright material.

The Publishers would be glad to hear from any unacknowledged copyright holders.

GU00802341

This book is one of a Framework series and is based upon and adapted from *The History Manual* by J. A. Cloake, V. Crinnion and S. M. Harrison, Framework Press, 1985, the first volume in the series.

First published 1988 by

Framework Press Educational Publishers Ltd.
St. Leonard's House
St. Leonardgate
Lancaster LA1 1NN

The Economics Manual: Skills at A and AS Level

ISBN 1 85008 041 0

Illustrations by Christopher Stephens

Cover design by John Angus

Typeset by Blackpool Typesetting Services Ltd., Blackpool

Printed by Redwood Burn Ltd., Trowbridge, Wiltshire

For Robert, Elizabeth, Martin, Lynn,
Kimberley and Natasha.

CONTENTS

		Page
INTRODUCTION		1
Chapter 1	**ANALYTICAL READING**	3
Chapter 2	**NOTE-MAKING**	31
Chapter 3	**ESSAY-WRITING**	55
Chapter 4	**HANDLING DATA**	89
Chapter 5	**MULTIPLE-CHOICE QUESTIONS**	121
Chapter 6	**PROJECTS**	129
Chapter 7	**REVISION**	141
Chapter 8	**THE EXAMINATION**	157

INTRODUCTION

Learning how to study effectively becomes more and more important as you progress through your studies. Therefore at Advanced level and beyond you need to spend time improving and developing your study skills. This book explains, discusses and demonstrates a range of basic skills required by Economics students. These skills are not confined to any one Economics examination and will therefore be useful to anyone studying syllabuses of any of the examination boards. This book will also be of use to you if you are studying Economics as part of another course.

Through the practice of the skills presented in *The Economics Manual* you will be able to develop your grasp of Economics, which is as much about the approach taken to the subject as about its content.

All too often students lack study skills, and thus remain dependent on notes dictated by the teacher, or prepare for the exam by rote-learning masses of information. Effective study at Advanced level involves gaining the confidence to think independently and critically. In time you will begin to generate your own ideas and interests. This book provides you with the skills to develop these interests, exchanging the role of diffident pupil for that of mature and enquiring student.

How to study?

How to Use This Book

Each chapter in this book concentrates on different skills which must be developed by the successful student. Nevertheless there are themes which run through the whole book. Active involvement, a critical attitude and identification of problems are amongst these. In every chapter there are examples to look at and exercises to do. You will be able to tackle all these exercises unaided after having read the appropriate parts of the book.

When looking at this book for the first time, you should use the skills of previewing and skimming discussed in the first chapter and look through the book to get a feel for its layout. The book follows a logical structure designed to complement the early stages of a study of Economics. Thus analytical reading is dealt with first, followed by a chapter on note-making, while the chapters on revision and the examination come at the end of the book. The book can be seen as a course in itself, or as a resource for the individual student to dip into as problems and weaknesses arise.

There are many examples and exercises contained in the book with significant Economics content. Many of them, therefore, provide a means of considering certain aspects of your work. A mixture of micro-economics and macro-economics is used. Some of you may disagree with some of the commentary associated with the examples and exercises. Such criticism should be seen as healthy. You will soon come to realise that there are very few clear-cut answers in Economics and that in time your own particular approach will be a matter of perspective. More important is that you develop a feeling for the many debates and disagreements associated with Economics which will need to be studied and critically appraised. It is hoped that using this book will aid that development.

ANALYTICAL READING

Page

A. **GENERAL PRINCIPLES** 4
   Gain a Proper Perspective 4
   Be Active 4
   Be Purposeful and Flexible 4
   Concentrate 7

B. **SPEED ADAPTED TO PURPOSE** 9

C. **SOURCES FOR READING** 10
   Books 10
      1. General Economics textbooks 11
      2. Subject-specific books 11
      3. Books of case-studies 11
      4. Other books 11
   Periodicals and Journals 11
   Newspapers and Magazines 12

D. **THE READING STRATEGY** 14
   A Summary of Stages, Reading Speeds and Purposes 14
   The Strategy 16
      1. The Preview 16
      2. The Overview 17
      3. The Inview 19
      4. Review and Recall 25

E. **CHECKLIST** 26

F. **END OF CHAPTER EXERCISE** 27

A. GENERAL PRINCIPLES

In order to gain a good grasp of the subject matter in Economics it will be necessary for you to do a lot of reading. For that time to be spent most productively you need to follow some general principles relating to analytical reading.

Gain a Proper Perspective

The general principle when approaching a new topic or book in Economics is to move from the general to the particular. This means that you should start by skimming the book in order to get some idea of what it contains and the order in which it appears, whilst establishing its relevance to your needs. In this way, information relating to the subject can be selected and absorbed *progressively*. You should try to get an overall perspective of the book so that you can perhaps refer to it at a later date when you are examining a different topic.

Be Active

A general theme of this book is that you should be active in all the studying you do. You should approach all types of reading in an *alert* and *critical* manner. You will be expected to question your findings and to *assimilate* them into what you already know. For this reason it is a good idea to read with a notebook at your side. You should jot down points which are new to you, which add something to your existing notes, or which make one aspect of a topic clearer. These notes must then be combined with your lesson notes (see Chapter 2).

It is a good idea to try to anticipate how the author is going to develop his argument. This requires your understanding of what has gone before and develops analytical skills. These are very important in Economics. Ask yourself questions about what the author is saying and if the book does not tell you everything you need, look at another text or consult your teacher. You should also be prepared to discuss your reading with others, especially where difficult or controversial points have been made.

Be Purposeful and Flexible

Do not apporach all Economics books in exactly the same way. Your approach will depend on the reason for reading the book.

Whenever you start reading, consider which of the following applies to your situation:

- Are you looking for general background knowledge?
- Are you looking for a specific answer to a question?
- Are you researching an essay topic?
- Are you seeking out the author's opinion?
- Are you seeking clarification of a particular topic?
- Are you checking your own understanding of a topic?

By keeping the purpose of your reading always in mind you will read more productively. Definition of your task in this way will determine the speed at which you read the information and the quantity of it that you will need to refer to.

In the same way you should be willing to vary your reading speed according to the difficulty of the ideas and language used. Some books will obviously be more difficult to read than others, but the difficulty of any text is relative to your existing knowledge and level of understanding of the topic. Thus the more productive and purposeful your reading, the easier it will get.

EXERCISE

(a) Read the following passage at your normal speed:

An economy may be analysed in terms of its constituent parts. These are often referred to as 'sectors'. The widest definition of these sectors is in terms of 'primary', 'secondary' and 'tertiary' (service) sectors. On the other hand, we can define sectors rather more narrowly, e.g. the engineering industries or the banking sector.

In this chapter we are interested in structural change in the U.K. economy and how this has affected the various sectors (broadly defined). Let us at the outset define these precisely under the following headings:

(a) *the primary sector* — includes activities directly related to natural resources, e.g. farming, mining

(b) *the secondary sector* — covers all goods produced from raw materials, including the processing of those raw materials. Manufacturing is the main element of this sector, which also includes construction and the public utility industries of gas, water and electricity

(c) *the tertiary sector* — includes all the private sector services, e.g. distribution, banking, insurance, and all the public sector services such as health and defence

Structural change means change in the relative size of the sectors. We may judge size by output or employment. Through time we would expect the structure of the economy to change. For instance, if economic growth occurs and people's incomes rise, then the demand for goods and services will rise generally, but will rise particularly in areas such as leisure services. Thus the expenditure on recreation, entertainment and educational services rose substantially between 1974 and 1984 from £10.8 bn. to £14.2 bn. (1980 prices).

Technical progress makes possible entirely new goods and services. New patterns of demand are thus created which in turn have an influence on structure. Other influences include availability of raw materials, the impact of international trade, and changes in taste.

If we take output as our measure of relative sector size, we find that the primary sector increased its share from 4.2% of output in 1973 to 9.5% in 1984, largely attributable to the growth in North Sea oil and gas. The secondary sector's share of output fell from a peak of 42% in 1964 to 31.8% in 1984. The tertiary sector's share of output has continually grown and now (1988) stands at around 60% of output.

(b) Now read the passage again in order to answer the following questions:

   (i) By how much did expenditure on recreation, entertainment and educational services rise between 1974 and 1984?

   (ii) Why can technical progress influence structure?

   (iii) Why has the output of the primary sector increased since 1973?

(c) Read the passage for a third time. This time ask yourself what influence on the structure of the economy the author sees as the most important.

Comment

(a) Your three readings should be done in very different ways. In the first reading you are assessing what material is contained in the passage and how it might be useful. In other words you should be gaining an overview of the subject matter.

(b) In your second reading you are looking for some specific material and it is likely that you have scanned through the material to find answers to the specific questions. You should find it useful that you have already assessed the content of the passage.

(c) Your third reading is the most difficult. You are looking for clues and different emphases which the author uses when discussing the various influences on the structure of the economy. You might like to discuss your findings with a fellow student to see if you come to the same conclusion.

Your three readings will have been executed at very different speeds. More of this later.

Concentrate

It is important in your study of Economics that you read widely and regularly, and bear in mind that your reading should always be productive. This will require a good level of concentration. You must learn to be aware of your own levels of concentration and the levels of concentration which are possible. Pull yourself up when your concentration lapses. Remember also that with practice and effort it is possible to improve your

own concentration. It can be helpful to arrange with other students to read a passage at the same time and discuss your conclusions.

The environment in which you read is very important. You should relieve yourself of any distractions and work where it is quiet and calm. Read for relatively short periods (say 30 minutes) and then give yourself a short break to rest your eyes and brain.

Problems with concentration?

SOME CAUSES	SOME SOLUTIONS
LACK OF PURPOSE	1. Define your task and actively seek out the relevant information. Take pleasure in ruthlessly ignoring irrelevant information! 2. Consult your teacher about what needs to be gained from reading about a particular topic.
LACK OF INTEREST	3. Approach the text in a more critical and/or imaginative manner. 4. Dull topics (e.g. tax revenue) can be made more palatable by viewing them in wider, more intriguing contexts (e.g. should we cut services in order to cut taxes?). 5. Challenge yourself to complete reading in fixed periods of time (but be realistic about the schedules you adopt!). 6. Reward yourself for meeting self-imposed targets or completing assignments (cups of tea, going out, etc.).
FATIGUE AND DISTRACTIONS	7. Discover your optimum time for reading/study—it varies from person to person (early morning? afternoon? late at night?). 8. Ensure your physical environment is conducive to serious analytical reading—quiet, warm and well-lit. 9. Take regular breaks (about every 20–30 minutes) for short periods (usually 5 minutes is enough—no longer). 10. Learn to recognise the signs of fatigue (slight eye-ache, mind-wandering, etc.).

from *The History Manual* (Framework Press, 1985) by J. A. Cloake, V. Crinnion and S. M. Harrison (Economics examples substituted).

When you read Economics books, remember that you should always be critical of content. This is particularly true when considering issues of government policy where Economics inevitably becomes associated with Politics. There is room for argument in Economics. The more involved you are able to get in the many debates the better your understanding of the subject will be and the more motivated you will become.

B. SPEED ADAPTED TO PURPOSE

Reading is a complex process and some students manage it better than others. But all students can become better readers by learning to use reading speeds strategically.

If you think back to the exercise on p.5, where you were asked to read the same extract about the structure of the economy several times, you will realise that not only did you approach each task in a different way but you read the extract at different speeds.

Look back at the exercise and consider the speed at which you approached each task. The third reading should have been the slowest and the second the fastest. This should have been a deliberate policy on your part. Analytical reading demands that you vary your speed of reading according to:
  (i) the difficulty of the material;
 (ii) the exact purpose for which you are reading the material;
(iii) how knowledgeable you are about the structure and content of the material.

These considerations are closely connected. The last reading was slower than the first two, despite your knowing what the purpose of the reading was and what was contained in the extract. In the third case you had to concentrate on every sentence the author wrote to look for the answer.

The second reading was the fastest because you knew the structure of the extract, the task was simple and specific and it was necessary only to *scan* most of the material until you reached key words and phrases.

A very important aspect of your Economics reading is comprehension. If you do not understand something the first time you read it, you should re-read it (perhaps a few times). If you still have problems, refer to a simpler textbook for help on the particular topic, or refer to a dictionary or a more specific dictionary of Economics.

You can calculate your own reading speed by using the following formula:

Reading speed (words per minute) =

$$\frac{\text{No. of pages read} \times \text{No. of words per average page}}{\text{No. of minutes spent reading}}$$

EXERCISE

Calculate your reading speed at different times of the day. You will need to choose texts of comparable difficulty, but do not use the same extract.

The following chart gives a very approximate idea of how reading speed relates to the task or purpose for reading. It relates to an 'average' student. You might find that you read rather more slowly or more quickly than the speeds suggested. In time you should become aware of your own 'gears' in relation to the level of difficulty of a text and the task. Thus practice becomes very important.

Average Standard	Speed (w.p.m.)	'Gear'	Expected Comprehension %	Purpose and Difficulty of Material
Slow	Less than 50	Crawl	100	Careful Studying (Very Difficult)
	100	Coasting	70–80	Reading for Meaning/ Pleasure/Information etc. (Easy/Normal Material)
Normal	200			
	300			
Fast	400	Racing	below 50	1. 'Overview' Skimming 2. Revision Learning: 1st stage of review
	500			
Exceptionally fast	600	Blur	below 10	1. 'Scanning' for Specific Words 2. Author's Arrangement of His Material and Ideas
	700			
	800			
	900			
	1000			
	up to			
	3000			

from *The History Manual* (Framework Press, 1985) by J. A. Cloake, V. Crinnion and S. M. Harrison.

C. SOURCES FOR READING

Your reading will be drawn from a number of different sources. We can categorise these into:
- books
- periodicals and journals
- newspapers and magazines

You will use all these sources at different times and in different ways, but the general principle should be to read widely.

Books

There is an extremely wide variety of Economics books available and this is growing all the time. You will soon discover that these books cover a range of topics and adopt many different approaches. Some are general textbooks which attempt to cover the whole of the Advanced level course; others just examine particular aspects. Some books are based on theory, others on the 'real world' or applied Economics. There are books which contain case studies for analysis and there are those which simply provide lists of questions for revision purposes and examination practice.

The study of Economics at Advanced level is not merely a process of collecting together facts and theories. It is largely concerned with the interpretation of observations in the economy. This requires the application of economic theory to the behaviour of individuals, groups and the whole economy.

The nature of Economics means that economists often disagree and therefore you will find that authors will often put different slants on the same subject matter. This is particularly true of texts of a more specialised nature.

1. GENERAL ECONOMICS TEXTBOOKS

General Economics textbooks try to give thorough coverage of the whole A level course, examining both economic theory and applied Economics. Inevitably these books are never short and the best approach will not be to read them through from cover to cover. It is unlikely that the books will follow the same structure as that adopted by your teacher in covering the course. You should therefore read chapters or sections of chapters where appropriate:
- as a brief introduction to a new topic
- as a source of additional notes while studying a topic
- as an aid to revision after completing a topic (see Chapter 7)

One great benefit of a large, comprehensive text is that it can act as a good source of reference where you can look up things you are unsure about and seek clarification.

2. SUBJECT-SPECIFIC BOOKS

These books tend to look at one area of Economics. You will usually be expected to have met the general principles contained in the book before and it is therefore useful to have a more general textbook at hand for reference. These specific books often contain rather more detail than the general ones and so are particularly useful when planning essays.

3. BOOKS OF CASE-STUDIES

Case-studies are designed to give practical illustrations of different issues in Economics. They are meant to be a stimulus to discussion and to provide a forum for the application of your knowledge to the real world. It is important for you to be able to apply your Economics and these books will provide you with plenty of practice.

4. OTHER BOOKS

There are other books ranging from simple introductions to Economics to books where the discussion of Economics arises from the analysis of data. Discuss with your teacher which books to use and find out what suitable books are stocked in the library.

Periodicals and Journals

It is increasingly useful in the study of Economics to be able to refer to periodicals and journals. These will provide you with up-to-date information on a variety of topics. Articles are generally quite short (between 3 and 20 pages) and deal with one aspect of your studies. The content of periodicals and journals can also provide you with some insight into economic debate. You will also be able to identify the range of topics about which economists are in debate.

Some of the most useful and accessible journals and periodicals are listed below: (Bank publications are usually free).

The Economic Review
National Westminster Bank Quarterly Review
Lloyds Bank Review
Lloyds Bank Economic Bulletin
Midland Bank Review
Economics (The journal of the Economics Association)

Although you have to pay for it, *The Economic Review* is probably the most useful of these. It is aimed specifically at the A level student and, as well as containing articles on topics of interest in Economics, it also has specimen essay questions with outline answers which you will find useful.

Information about *The Economic Review* is available from:

Philip Allan Publishers Limited,
Market Place,
Deddington, Oxford OX5 4SE

Newspapers and Magazines

Newspapers and magazines provide you with an excellent source of up-to-date material on issues relating to the economy. You should get into the habit of reading a quality newspaper, such as *The Guardian, The Independent, The Times* and *The Daily Telegraph*. Some of these run regular articles relating specifically to Economics which can be very helpful in your studies. It is often a good idea to keep a scrap-book of articles which can then be used when you are studying particular topics.

When reading newspapers or magazines, be aware of any political bias displayed in the articles. So long as you are aware of this you will not be misled. It is only the unwary, who are unable to distinguish between fact and opinion, who fall into traps.

EXAMPLE

Below is a passage about government economic policy.

(a) Read it carefully and decide whether or not you consider it to be biased.

> Government economic policy in the 1980s has proved to be a great success. The government's main aim was to bring down inflation which it has done admirably. Growth in the latter part of the 80s has been above the average of the U.K.'s main competitors. Allied to this, there has been a reduction in numbers unemployed. This turn-around in the economy has been due to a reliance on sound monetary policy and in particular to the Medium Term Financial Strategy. The economy is now on target and is set to make a significant contribution to world prosperity in the 1990s.

(b) Note the following hints about what to look for and read the passage again. What do you think now?
  (i) Is there anything in the passage which is untrue?
  (ii) Have words been used which over-stress a point?
  (iii) Do you consider that only half the story has been told in places?
  (iv) Have claims been made which are really only opinions?

(c) Finally, read these comments made about the passage:

The passage has obviously been written so as to enable you to spot bias. You would rarely read such a passage in a quality newspaper. It is interesting to note, however, that nothing in the passage is untrue. Stress has been put on some aspects rather than others. This means that the uninformed reader gets only half the story.

Note in particular the use of the words 'admirably' and 'sound' which convey a feeling of approval and achievement. Also note that, although it is claimed that inflation has fallen, the passage does not discuss the cost of this in terms of numbers unemployed. Furthermore, the passage indicates that unemployment is falling but does not indicate the very high levels it reached before this began to happen.

EXERCISE

The following passage is written from a very different viewpoint. Using the same hints as before, compare and contrast it to the one above. Note that nothing contained in either passage is untrue.

> Government policy in the 1980s has not proved to be a great success. Inflation has been brought down, but only at a great cost to the unemployed. Throughout long periods of the 1980s our growth rate has been slower than that of our major competitors. Unemployment figures rose dramatically in the first half of the decade. This poor performance has been due to an over-reliance on monetary policy and in particular the Medium Term Financial Strategy. The economy is unlikely to do much better in the 1990s.

D. THE READING STRATEGY

To get the most from your reading you should approach it in a strategic way. There are four main parts or stages in a successful reading strategy. Each has a specific purpose, the importance of which will depend on the source of the reading and whether or not you know what you are looking for beforehand. Each stage may require different reading speeds, but they will all demand an active approach. The main purpose of the strategy is to provide you with a method of identifying and extracting information in an accurate and efficient way. The process discussed here may seem rather long and complicated at first but you may find that you do much of it anyway without realising it. It is worth trying the whole process since you will soon become familiar with it. In the long run it will save you much time and effort.

A Summary of Stages, Reading Speeds and Purposes

STAGE	SPEED	PURPOSE
1. Preview: knowing what you want	—	1. To define your reading purpose. 2. To generate questions that you hope the book will answer.
2. Overview: discovering what you want	Skimming	1. To establish how relevant and useful the book is going to be. 2. To give you an idea about the structure of the book and how you might approach it. 3. To "trigger off" connections with your existing knowledge, making you more sensitive to the material at hand. 4. To give you an idea about: (a) the difficulty of the text (b) its scholarly stature.
3. Inview: understanding and selecting what you want	Careful reading	1. To discover the main points, either (a) of the book or (b) for your reading task. 2. To separate the subordinate points. 3. To extract the relevant information.
4. Review/ Recall: assimilating what you have got	Skimming/ re-reading selected passages	1. To confirm that (a) all the main points have been correctly identified and understood (b) your initial question-framework was valid and has been satisfied. 2. To encourage the filtering and re-ordering of information. 3. To reinforce recall of the main information.

Adapted from p.27, *The History Manual* (Framework Press, 1985) by J. A. Cloake, V. Crinnion and S. M. Harrison

SOME HINTS

(i) Before you begin, make sure you have the following to hand:
- Plenty of paper for brief notes and page references
- Pencil and pen
- A general dictionary and a dictionary of Economics terms

(ii) Ensure that your environment is free from distractions and allows a good level of concentration.

(iii) Take short breaks at regular intervals.

(iv) Position your text as below (A) rather than the usual position (B). You will find it more comfortable.

A

B

The Strategy

1. THE PREVIEW

This stage is all about knowing what the purpose of your reading is to be. It pre-determines what you hope to get from your source and how you approach it.

EXERCISE

Take a topic which you have studied or which you are studying at the moment. Think about your reading associated with this topic and provide yourself with a written preview for this topic.

The following questions might help you:

(a) Do I want to read about the whole topic or just one aspect of it?

(b) What sorts of things do I need to get out of the reading which will help my understanding and supplement my notes?

(c) What questions can I ask of myself which I would hope the reading will satisfy? See *The Inview* (p.19).

(d) What source or sources am I going to read?

(e) How long do I have available for this task?

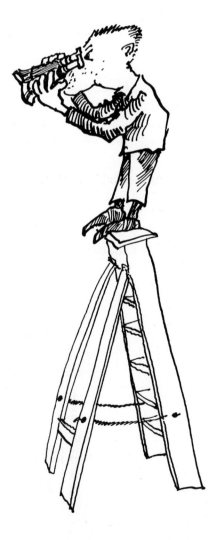

2. THE OVERVIEW

You may consider that the overview wastes time but, in fact, more than any other stage of the strategy, it actually saves time. The overview provides you with a survey of the book which will give you a feel for its content and style. This in turn will help you when it comes to looking for specific information to answer the questions you have set yourself in the preview.

Part of your overview will consist of skimming and sampling the source:

Skimming entails looking for familiar words and phrases and paying particular attention to headings and sub-headings. You should try to gain a general sense of the structure of the book.

Sampling provides you with a guide to the style and difficulty of the book. It is particularly useful to sample the beginnings and ends of chapters. If it is an article which you wish to study, sample the conclusion. This should give you some idea of just how useful the information within it should be.

What to look out for
We will concentrate in this section on what to look out for when overviewing a book. Many of the principles are equally useful when looking at other sources, however. It is worth stressing yet again that you will gain more from this process if you approach it in an active and positive manner.

(a) Title page
You should be able to get an idea of the scope and coverage of an Economics book from its title. Many Economics books are just called *Economics*, and, as you would expect, they are general in their coverage. It is often difficult to know at what level they are pitched. A book with the title *An Introduction to Economics* will normally be an introduction to the subject aimed at students who have never studied it before, but what about a book titled *Economics: A Student's Guide*?

Economics books which are not general in their coverage should make this clear in their titles. You can expect *Economics of the Real World*, for example, to be a book applying theoretical economic perspectives to real world situations. Other books aiming at partial coverage might include *Introduction to Micro-economics* or *Macro-economics* or *Case-Studies in Regional Economics*.

Generally the narrower the title of a book, the more specific it is, and therefore the more difficult it will be. Thus it is not likely that a book entitled *Managerial Economics: A Mathematical Approach* will be much use at A level.

(b) Publishers' blurb
Some idea of the main subject(s) of a book can be found on its back cover. This should indicate to you the scope and coverage of the book. Look out for abstracts from reviews of previous editions of the book which the publisher will often include. These will emphasise the strengths of the book, but remember that the publisher would never draw attention to a poor review.

(c) Table of contents
This important section will tell you what the book covers and, if chapters are subdivided, how much detail is provided. It will show you the organisation of the book and convey which areas the author sees as most important. Do not assume that if a topic is not cited in the contents it is not covered. It may well be embedded within another section. For this reason you should also consult the index. If you see certain chapters or sections which particularly interest you, or you think might be useful, you can then turn to them for sampling.

Notice particularly the structure of chapters in general Economics textbooks. You will find that most of them cover micro-economic concepts first, followed by macro-economics. Any study of the international economy is usually left until last. Some textbooks do provide alternatives to this and the coverage in these books is often very different from that in the more traditional book. When reading you should attempt to compare and contrast these two different styles.

(d) The index
Most books contain an alphabetical listing of the topics covered in the book, and the pages on which they occur. Indexes vary in quality and accuracy and you will soon discover which books you can rely on. It is particularly important in a general Economics textbook that the index has a very wide coverage. As well as using the index to find answers to particular questions and queries you can gain some idea of the usefulness of the book from it.

EXERCISE

Take a general textbook and assess the quality of the index by looking up the following terms. The terms get more specific as the list goes on. Most general texts will contain reference to the first few. Only the better ones will contain reference to most of them.

- Supply
- Money
- Inflation
- Investment
- Inferior goods
- Growth
- Exports
- Exchange rates
- Complements
- Barriers to Entry

- Classical unemployment
- Comparative advantage
- Oligopoly
- Protectionism
- Expectations
- Forward Markets
- Buffer stocks
- Rational expectations
- Deadweight losses
- Goodhart's Law

(e) Synopses

Some books have a synopsis at the beginning of each chapter. This is particularly useful when you are trying to get a feel for the content of the chapter. Often it will provide you with an idea of whether to continue and read the chapter or whether to look elsewhere for the answers to your questions.

(f) Summaries and Checklists

At the ends of chapters or sections, authors often provide summaries or checklists of the important points and principles contained in the chapters. If these are done well, they can save you having to scan the whole chapter to gain some idea of its content. Summaries and checklists can also help you when you are doing revision reading. By working through a checklist you can ascertain whether you do understand important points and concepts.

(g) Prefaces

Books will often have a preface, foreword or introduction. Sections of these are often written specifically for the student and will give you an idea of how the author intends you to use the book and suggestions for getting the most from it. The author will often tell you at what level the book is pitched (e.g. GCSE level, A level or first year degree level, etc.), and the range and scope of the book. If the book is written in an attempt to support a particular principle this will also be made clear.

Successful skimming and sampling of a book

Even if you have already decided on the usefulness or otherwise of a particular book, it is good practice to skim through it. The reader about to abandon the book may find new information not included in the contents or index. The reader who thinks the book suitable may find that his/her first impressions are confirmed, or the skimming may prove disappointing so that the decision has to be re-assessed.

Pay particular attention to tables and diagrams in the book. These can often provide you with more information and more of an insight into the book than a whole page of words. This is also worth remembering when you come to write.

Skimming should be done very quickly (a few seconds per page). Try to find the main points rather than worrying about precise content and concepts at this stage. You may wish to sample some sections during the skimming process. Sampling will be done at normal speed in order to gain a feeling for the style, quality and difficulty of the book.

If you are already aware of the organisation of the book by reference to the contents, the whole process of skimming and sampling will be much easier.

Once your overview is complete, you should have determined the relative usefulness of the text. You should also have an idea of the best way of tackling it, and of what else you should be looking for which will complement or add something to the text.

EXERCISE

Carry out an overview of a general introductory Economics textbook. Follow the guidelines presented above. When you have carried out a full overview, answer the following questions.

(a) Has the author recommended a particular approach?
(b) Do you consider this to be a sensible approach for you?
(c) How good is the index provided?
(d) Does the book follow the traditional micro-macro structure?
(e) How much additional material are you likely to need to accompany this book?
(f) How difficult is the book?

3. THE INVIEW

At this stage you are looking for answers to the questions you set yourself during the Preview (p.16). This will involve you in much more careful reading and analysis. Relevant sections should be read thoroughly and critically. It may be necessary to read a paragraph more than once. Often it is a good idea to read the whole section more than once. For more difficult books this will certainly aid understanding. Once you feel confident that you have selected the appropriate information you should make notes on the important points and concepts. Your reading will lead you to ask more questions, which should be noted. These will often form the basis of another block of reading.

(a) What are the main points?

Analytical reading demands that you should be able to understand and select the main points from a particular text. This really is central to your task. You cannot make good notes until this is mastered.

In a general Economics textbook there will be many themes running through the whole work.

As soon as you deal with individual chapters or other sources of information, however, ideas will become more concrete. The main ideas will usually be expressed in the synopsis (if there is one), or in the conclusion or summary. Look carefully at first and last paragraphs as well.

Each paragraph of text should also have a main point. The best authors follow this sort of pattern throughout their books, and with practice you will recognise their style, which will make your reading easier.

(b) Looking for clues

There will often be visual clues within the text. Look at the way we have made use of capitals, italics and bold type to make certain things stand out in this book. The visual clues may also include the use of asterisks or bullet points, the number or lettering of points, and underlining.

Verbal clues are often helpful. When an author wishes to qualify, stress or contradict a point, he/she will use words such as 'firstly', 'furthermore', 'therefore', 'however', 'equally', 'since' and 'on the other hand'.

Main ideas will often be signalled by use of words or phrases such as 'significant', 'it is obvious that', 'thus', 'fundamental', 'the main point being' and 'leads to'.

(c) Filling in the important details

Once you have recognised the main point of a particular chapter, section or article, your next task is to fill in the important details. You should look for explanation of the main point, and analysis or examples which make use of it.

The question you must ask yourself is how much you should include in your notes. This will be considered in more detail in the next chapter.

Generally you should include:
  (i) those ideas which are central to the economist's argument;
 (ii) examples and analyses which successfully illustrate the main points;
(iii) any underlying theory which is central to the idea;
 (iv) any new terms and concepts which you have not already come across.

EXAMPLE

On pages 21 and 22 there are examples of a preview and an overview of a book. The book is C. D. Cohen (ed.), *Agenda For Britain 1: Micro Policy* (Philip Allan, 1982). These are followed by an example of an inview which deals with the chapter on the Economic Implications of Micro-electronics.

EXERCISE

Carry out a preview, overview and inview of the extract about nationalised industries on pp.23 to 25. When you have done that, consider the following questions:
  (a) Did the structure of the extract help with your overview? Why?
  (b) Which part or parts of the extract were particularly difficult to follow? How did you overcome this during your inview?
  (c) Which questions from your preview have been left unanswered?
  (d) What further questions have been stimulated by the extract?
  (e) How will you go about answering these questions?

AN EXAMPLE OF THE STRATEGY IN PRACTICE

AGENDA FOR BRITAIN 1: MICRO POLICY (C.D. COHEN (ed.))

I. PREVIEW

1. Written by a number of economists (experts)
2. Range of applied topics with government policies?
3. How up to date?
4. Illustrate areas of conflict and debate. How political?

II. OVERVIEW

Published in 1982. Looks at micro policy in topical areas including impact of micro-electronics.
Influential authors?

Table of contents   7 chapters, all contemp. topics.
      Industrial performance, Micro-electronics, Energy, Taxation, Trade Unions, Social Policy, Housing.

Preface   First of 2 volumes (2nd on Macro Policy)
"Govt. policy should not be based on ideology - careful analysis is required."

Index   Quite short but clear. Many references to taxation - not surprising. References to authors as well as topics.

Notes   Many notes at end of each chapter - perhaps further reading but look a bit 'academic'.

Overall   Chapters quite long; difficult in places.
Good for background information.
Plenty of diagrams and tables.
Quick scan on Ch. 2 (Microelectronics) reveals some interesting diagrams. Much on investment. Looks at area of invention and innovation.

Chapter 2. THE ECONOMIC IMPLICATIONS OF MICRO-ELECTRONICS

PAGE	MAIN POINTS	QUESTIONS/ REFERENCES
p.57	Every industry and service activity has been affected to some extent by the micro-electronics revolution.	
p.58	Micro-electronics industry divided into 3 main sectors: i) Consumer electronics ii) Electronic capital goods iii) Electronic components	Military equipment??
p.59	Defence electronics accounts for 1/4 of all the O/P of the micro-electronics industry	
p.62	With completely new products it can take up to 30 years for the majority of firms or households to adopt.	Examples? Robots?
p.64	n.b. table is v. useful.	
p.84	The introduction of new technology might be a destabilising process.	Schumpeter via unemployment
p.85	The slower growth of the world economy in the 1970's was partly due to a shift in the pattern of investment away from capacity expansion towards replacement.	
p.85	Labour-saving processes have undoubtedly created unemployment, but innovations are likely to create an overall expansion in demand and generate new employment opportunities.	Statistics? When?

NATIONALISED INDUSTRIES

Introduction

In this section we are going to examine aspects of nationalised industries and their role in the UK economy. Before we do so, however, it is important to be clear exactly what constitutes a nationalised industry. There are three main features of a nationalised industry which are:

(a) Its assets are in public ownership.
(b) Its revenue is mainly derived from the sale of goods and services.
(c) Its Board is appointed by a government minister, but its members are not civil servants.

Examples of nationalised industries include British Rail, British Coal and the Post Office.

The Importance of Nationalised Industries

Nationalised industries are very large organisations. For example, they account for about 12% of total employment and around 10% of national output. But because they supply vital materials and provide important transport networks, their significance is greater than is indicated by these figures.

The Reasons for Nationalisation

Nationalisation occurs for both economic and political reasons. It is perhaps in this area in particular that the distinction between Economics and Politics becomes most blurred. Essentially we can pin-point five major reasons for nationalisation:

(i) *To prevent the abuse of monopoly power*
Large firms which are able to dominate a market or industry will often not operate in the public interest when their first objective is to make profits. Indeed, it is often the case that in these circumstances consumers will be exploited. In order to prevent this type of exploitation, the monopoly firm can be taken into public ownership. In this way the government can control the pricing policies of the firm.

(ii) *To aid the redistribution of income*
If, following nationalisation, prices are reduced and wages increased, there is a redistribution of income away from the producer towards the consumer and the worker. Since the producer was formerly a private concern, this implies a reduction in income going to shareholders. Once the government has control of the pricing strategy of the firm, it is also able to subsidise goods if it wishes, redistributing income from taxpayers to consumers.

(iii) *To increase economic efficiency*
Clause 4 of the Labour Party's constitution gives as an aim:
> *To secure for the workers by hand or by brain the full fruits of their industry and the most equitable distribution thereof that may be possible upon the basis of the common ownership of the means of production, distribution and exchange, and the best obtainable system of popular administration and control of each industry or service.*

The aim is to bring the means of production, distribution and exchange into public ownership in order to increase economic efficiency. It is argued that this is achieved because an industry under unified control is easier to organise and monitor and because there will be benefits from economies of scale.

Economic efficiency can also be increased by elimination of duplication; in other words, by organising production so that there is no wastage due to overlapping activities. The supply of electricity requires the provision of 'channels' of supply and a competitive industry may mean wasteful duplication of these 'channels'. It is more efficient just to provide one set of wiring for a given area.

(iv) *To maintain employment*
This objective of public ownership gains popularity at times of high unemployment. Once again it is profit-maximising firms who may not wish to employ extra labour. Bringing a firm into public ownership means that the profit motive is not so important, and other objectives, such as the provision of full employment, can be adopted.

(v) *To ensure the adequate supply of goods and services*
There are some goods in relation to which the private market on its own would result in under-provision. Take the example of national defence. If this were to be left to individuals and private firms to organise, then whereas some people would contribute towards national defence, others would choose to be free-riders, not paying their way and relying on others to contribute. This in turn would result in an under-provision of the good. Thus, to take a firm into public ownership and to instruct it to make certain goods to be paid for from the public purse is the only way round the problem. Firms supplying defence products may also be nationalised for reasons of national security of course.

There may also be an inadequate supply of some goods and services, where the required investment in an enterprise is so high that it may not be undertaken by private individuals. Take the example of the building of a nuclear power station. Would private individuals be willing to invest in such an expensive project where the returns might only become apparent years after the original investment?

The Performance of Nationalised Industries

It is perhaps unfair to compare the performance of nationalised industries with that of the private sector, because the structure of a nationalised industry is very different and because nationalised industries often pursue different objectives from private, profit-maximising enterprises. On the other hand, there is evidence to lead us to believe that the performance of the nationalised industries has been poor. Some of this evidence is listed below:

(a) Earnings and prices have tended to rise more rapidly in nationalised industries than in other industries.

(b) Despite the greater rise in prices, profits in the nationalised industries have been lower than those in the private sector.

(c) Internal investment in nationalised industries has been low compared with that in the private sector.

Summary

Whilst there are good reasons for having nationalised industries, their performance, although not strictly comparable with that of private industries, has been poor. In particular, although nationalised industries are not expected to maximise profits, they have not generally made sufficient profits to provide for full internal reinvestment and have had to rely on government subsidies.

It may be possible to achieve some of the objectives of nationalisation by other means. For example, a system of licensing might be adopted, whereby the right to supply a certain product is given to an individual firm.

4. REVIEW AND RECALL

This final stage of your reading strategy is very important. You cannot expect to understand everything at once, but you must review and recall your work throughout your studies. That applies to this book as much as to any other.

Review

Reviewing material also helps you to summarise main points in preparation for note-making. The processing and filtering of material will reinforce the main points which, ultimately, you must remember.

You should re-read relevant sections of books and articles periodically to make sure you have not missed anything. On each reading your recall of it will increase, but so should your understanding of it, particularly if it is a text which you first read at the beginning of your course.

Recall

Most people forget about 80% of what they have read within about twenty-four hours, and more as time continues. Thus it is vital that over a period you slowly build up the amount of material which you are able to recall. It will greatly assist both your understanding of Economics and your long-term recall if you make a habit of trying to remember the main points and concepts.

When you have completed the process of review you should put your notes and book aside and go through the main points until you know them thoroughly. Recall is invaluable because it will keep you active and help improve your concentration.

Review and recall are dealt with in more detail in Chapter 7.

EXERCISE

Return to the beginning of this chapter and apply the strategy of preview, overview, inview, and review and recall. To what extent are you using the advice offered here? Applying the strategy will help you to ensure that you have mastered the main ideas in the chapter. This is a crucial activity and links into the next chapter on note-making. The review/recall stage will determine how successful you have been in your reading.

E. CHECKLIST √ √ √ √ √ √ √ √ √ √ √

1	Use a range of sources of information when studying.
2	When beginning a new topic, consult a general Economics textbook before attempting more specialised reading.
3	When tackling a new source of information, start with a preview, followed by an overview.
4	Spend time deciding precisely what information you are looking for in a particular book or article.
5	Be active in your approach at all times.
6	Read for periods of such a length that your concentration does not lapse. Take regular short breaks.
7	Make use of the preview, overview, inview, review/recall strategy. It might seem a lengthy process at first but in time you will find it very worthwhile.

This?

Or this?

F. END OF CHAPTER EXERCISE

Read through the following passage, using the skills of analytical reading you have learned about in this chapter:

What is Economics About Anyway?

Economics is a study of the ways in which people provide for their wants and needs. Economists are concerned with the ways in which people apply their efforts to natural resources in order to satisfy wants. People work so that they can obtain more of the things they want and thus it is wants rather than needs which provide the dominant motives for economic activity.

Whilst everybody has needs for survival, it is very difficult to define need in terms of any particular quantity of a commodity. If we tried to do this, it would imply that a certain level of consumption was 'right' for the individual. This in turn would involve a value judgement, which economists generally try to avoid. Unfortunately, since resources are limited, it is not possible for everybody to have everything they want. Thus we have a basic economic problem which can be stated simply as: infinite wants, limited resources.

Most resources have alternative uses. Thus if we use them up producing one good, we cannot use them to produce another. Thus the real cost of producing one good is the lost opportunity of producing its alternative, or at least the next best alternative. The real cost of producing, say, six cars, is the bus which could alternatively have been produced. This view of costs is termed by economists the opportunity cost.

Therefore Economics is about solving the problem of how best to maximise the level of economic welfare, given limited resources. We are interested in deciding what should be done and what should be left undone, what quantities of each good to produce and how, and how to distribute the goods produced so as to satisfy the maximum number of people. All societies face these problems, but many have rather different solutions to them. In every society, individual consumers, institutions and the government all exert some influence. One of the differences between countries is the amount of influence various groups have on these choices.

Looking at the different political and social structures which exist in the world today, and the way in which these systems have developed, we may be tempted to think that we are making use of a wide variety of economic systems. However, apart from small groups of people who still lead traditional, often tribal, existences, where most things are done through tradition, there are essentially only two alternative systems.

. . . *continued*

THE TWO ALTERNATIVE SYSTEMS

The first of these can be termed the capitalist system, although it is also referred to as the free market system or market economy. Here, the state plays only a very small part in economic activity and most interactions within the economy are done via a complex system of trades commonly described as the market mechanism or price mechanism. The price mechanism is used for allocating resources to various uses by pricing each good or service in the economy. Producers, given the price of a product, decide how much to supply and consumers decide how much to buy at that price. If more is demanded than is supplied, then price rises to equate the two. Movements in prices therefore bring about changes in the ways in which society uses its scarce resources. The price mechanism allocates goods and services to consumers according to consumers' willingness to pay. Thus, if there is a shortage of a particular good, those who are willing to pay most for the good receive it. Naturally, therefore, those with the most purchasing power have an advantage over those with less when it comes to the allocation of goods. This has led some economists to suggest that where there are large differences in people's incomes, the system is unfair.

A second method of solving the economic problem is one by which solutions are worked out by central agencies which then impose those solutions on producers and consumers. This is known as a command economy or planned economy. A fully planned economy is one where all the important means of production are publicly owned. Often the logic of public ownership is based upon the desire for a more equitable distribution of income and wealth. Here, if there is a shortage of a good, rather than those with the most purchasing power being able to buy it, it is often those most willing to stand in queues who get it.

In the 'real world' we do not see pure forms of the capitalist economy or the planned economy. In the Western world, often seen as the most capitalist, we observe significant intervention by governments, for example. They often intervene to modify the operation of market forces. For example, the market mechanism is unlikely to provide a credible national defence for a country if it relies on people's willingness to pay. Thus the government taxes people in order to provide such goods.

. . . continued

ECONOMICS AS A SCIENCE

Much debate centres around the extent to which Economics is a science. Economists claim to be able to understand and predict certain aspects of human behaviour with some accuracy, and therefore Economics is often termed a social science. But the success of any science rests on the ability of scientists to separate their views of what does happen from what they would like to happen. The ability to do this is based partly on knowing the difference between positive and normative statements.

Positive and Normative Statements

A positive statement is one which deals with facts. If a disagreement arises over a positive statement, it can be settled by looking at facts and seeing whether or not they support the statement. Positive statements must therefore either be true or false. In other words they must either be consistent with facts or refutable by them.

A normative statement includes or implies words such as 'ought'. For example, 'unemployment figures ought to be lower' is a normative statement. Such statements reflect people's attitudes and are based on value judgements. Unlike positive statements, normative statements cannot be verified by looking at the facts. No one is suggesting, however, that economists should not express normative judgements. Indeed they have every right to do so, as everybody has.

A scientific approach is confined to positive statements. It deals with questions which arise from those statements and it attempts to provide answers to them by looking at the evidence. In trying to answer questions, Economics can make use of the scientific approach common to all sciences. One of the major objectives is, therefore, to develop theories, which are general statements describing and explaining the relationships between things we observe in the real world.

Scientific Method

Scientific method is aimed at helping to build such theories. There are four steps involved in scientific method:

1. We must define any concept which is used in such a way that it can be measured with some accuracy.
2. We must formulate an hypothesis. This is a tentative, untested statement, which attempts to explain how our concepts are related. Hypotheses are based on observations and assumptions.
3. We must test our hypothesis and make predictions.
4. We must test the hypothesis to see if its predictions are consistent with the facts. In the natural sciences this involves laboratory experiments, but in the social sciences, where the real world is our laboratory, we must test the hypothesis by recourse to the behaviour of human society. If our hypothesis is supported by the evidence, then we have a successful theory.

. . . *continued*

CONCLUSION

Economic analysis is generally based on the procedures above. The extent to which the economist uses scientific method will determine how scientific we can regard the subject as being. The subject matter of Economics is, however, human behaviour, and this is far less predictable than the behaviour of inanimate matter. Thus, the economist cannot achieve the precision of the natural scientist. But the fact that humans are different does not pose as many problems as one might expect. Although individuals often act in unpredictable ways, we find that groups of individuals, especially when large, do act in a rather more predictable fashion.

It is often claimed that Economics cannot be scientific because economists never agree on economic policies. But these disputes are often the result of inadequacies of information generally or differences in political ideology specifically. Since policies often involve normative elements we would expect there to be significant disagreement. Indeed, the debate surrounding the study of Economics is healthy. We should always question what is going on around us and the intense debate that this sometimes causes in Economics just makes it a more exciting subject to study.

Here's hoping that you find your study of Economics as exciting as it really is!

NOTE-MAKING

		Page
A.	WHY MAKE NOTES?	32
B.	WHAT IS NOTE-MAKING ABOUT?	32
C.	WHAT TO MAKE NOTES ON	38
	The Subject Matter	38
	The Task	38
D.	ALTERNATIVE NOTE-MAKING METHODS	41
	Linear Notes	41
	Pattern Notes	42
	Spider Notes	44
	Tables and Charts	46
	Card Indexes	49
E.	SUMMARY	51
F.	CHECKLIST	52
G.	END OF CHAPTER EXERCISE	53

A. WHY MAKE NOTES?

1. Notes are at the centre of your study of Economics. All your study activities are based on note-making, and in particular your notes will help you:
   —get the most from your own reading;
   —get the most from your lessons;
   —remember important facts and concepts;
   —analyse data;
   —write essays;
   —revise for examinations.

2. A good set of notes will act as a reference both for study and for revision, so it is important that your notes are of high quality. Making good notes as you progress through your course will help your understanding of Economics. It will also save you time and work in the long run.

B. WHAT IS NOTE-MAKING ABOUT?

Note-making is a very personal process. But the idea behind it is:
—to understand the subject matter;
—to select what is important;
—to organise that information in a form which is easily legible, easy to refer to and easy to remember.

One common mistake is to write too much. This means it is often difficult to find the information you are looking for at a later date and it can easily become confused in your mind. On the other hand, you should avoid writing too little so that it is difficult to remember what your notes are about when you come to revise.

However you decide to make notes, the following principles should be taken into account:

1. Devise a scheme of note-making which suits your needs. Let it develop as you become more used to making notes until you have a

personal system. You might need some time to experiment with different methods. Try this until you are happy with your scheme.

2. Do not copy from books and periodicals. Copying unchanged information will not help your understanding. You should re-think the text in your own mind and write concise notes on it in the style and vocabulary which you would normally use. If a phrase is particularly useful, you ought to write it in quotation marks and note the author and source. Consider two people who are making notes from a book. Person A copies everything word for word. She reads a sentence, it briefly enters the memory and the brain co-ordinates the motor skills which move the pen to write the sentence down. Person B starts by reading the sentence. She then thinks about what it means. If it is considered to be relatively important, it is concisely reformulated using her own vocabulary and pen is put to paper. Who will have the greater understanding and recall at the end of the exercise?

   Eventually, you should seek to have a single set of notes, so be prepared to update and rewrite your initial work. This in itself will help understanding and memory, and further cut down the work you will need to do at revision time. It is far more productive to spend your revision period learning your notes and practising skills than to be rewriting your notes into a form which makes sense.

3. Do not attempt to write down everything your teacher says in a lesson. If you try to do this, it is easy to get left behind and miss a sentence which is important. Develop a style which allows you to listen both to the teacher and to any discussion which ensues, whilst at the same time noting important points. The use of abbreviations (discussed below) can help here. On the other hand, if your teacher does talk rather too quickly or you miss a point, speak up. Others will undoubtedly be in the same position.

4. Make your notes clear and legible. Your notes need to be ordered and accurate and reflect the subject matter being dealt with. You can memorise material more easily when it is presented clearly. The following ideas and styles may help you organise your ideas and information:

HEADINGS—These should be used to divide your notes into sections of manageable length. Your headings should represent the content of the notes which follow, so make sure the heading is accurate. Headings should stand out in some way, so that your notes can be scanned when you are looking for a particular piece of information. You can use capitals, underlining, colour and highlighting, boxing in, etc. to make headings easily visible.

NUMBERING OF POINTS—This has the dual advantage of further structuring your work and helping you to remember all the points about a topic. For example, knowing that there are three points to remember about a particular topic means that you are less likely to miss out points when it comes to writing an essay.

ACRONYMS—These are words formed from initials. For example UNESCO stands for the United Nations Educational Scientific and Cultural Organisation. Some people find it easy to remember points in the form of an acronym by taking one letter to represent a point and then forming a word from the letters. This can be built into your notes and used for revision purposes. If you think this could be useful, try it out.

SPACING AND INDENTING—These can improve the visual quality and clarity of your notes. Do not cram too many notes onto a page, as it will be difficult to find points at a later stage. It is also useful to indent your work so that lists, quotes or important points stand out. If you stick to a particular system here, your notes will be ordered.

CAPITALS AND EMPHASES—Key words or phrases or important economic concepts can be underlined or written in capital letters to make them stand out.

EXAMPLE

Look at the specimen page of notes on Economic Development on p.34. Notice the use that has been made of headings, underlining, numbering, and indenting, and pick out the important economic concept which is part of point 2.

ECONOMIC DEVELOPMENT POLICIES   from Smith p. 76-9

1. <u>Economic Planning</u>
   - fully-planned, centrally-controlled economy
   - but most developed countries have grown with very little govt. assistance.

2. <u>Educational Policy</u>
   Under-education is a serious barrier to development.
   How should educational funds be spent?
      (i) eradicating illiteracy
      (ii) technical training/specialisation?
   The problem is that education spending is expensive and the benefits very long-term.
   It has a very high <u>opportunity cost</u>.

3. <u>Population Control</u>
   To win the race between incr. pop'n and incr. income a country can either:
      (i) create Y growth > pop'n growth;
   or (ii) control pop'n growth.
   (ii) is probably easier than (i) but note problems of religion and custom.

4. <u>Capital Acquisition</u>
   Acquire funds for development via
      (i) savings of domestic h/h and firms
      (ii) loans from abroad
      (iii) contributions from foreigners
      (iv) multinationals

DIAGRAMS, CHARTS AND TABLES—These are all very important in Economics. Many ideas are best represented in diagrammatic form and indeed are difficult to explain without reference to a diagram or a table. When it comes to drawing diagrams, there are a number of important things to remember:

(i) Diagrams should be large and clear.

(ii) Accuracy is very important.

(iii) Every diagram should have a title.

(iv) Lines should be clearly labelled.

(v) There should be appropriate use of light shading.

(vi) The diagram should be explained in the text you are writing.

(vii) You should refer to the diagram in your work.

(viii) Appropriate abbreviations should be used to avoid cluttering the diagram.

(ix) Axes should be clearly labelled.

(x) Colour should be used where it can make the diagram clearer.

USING ABBREVIATIONS—This will mean that you can take notes faster and more efficiently. You can develop your own system, but there are a number of general abbreviations and abbreviations peculiar to Economics which you might like to use. Use abbreviations consistently in your notes, but remember that they should never be used in essays, unless forming part of a mathematical equation. Below are two lists of abbreviations which you should find helpful:

General Abbreviations	Definitions
>	greater than
<	less than
△	change in
vv.	vice-versa
ff.	following
→	follows on/leads to
∵	because
∴	therefore
≡	identical to
ch.	chapter
govt.	government
⇒	implies

Abbreviations Used in Economics	Definitions
U	unemployment
W	wages
w	wage rate
Y	income or output
C	consumption
I	investment
G	government spending
r or i	interest rates
M^s	money supply
M^d	demand for money
h/h	households
eqm.	equilibrium
D	demand
S	supply
B of P	balance of payments
B of E	Bank of England
X	exports
M	imports
T	taxation
t	rate of tax

Abbreviations Used in Economics	Definitions
MC	marginal cost
MR	marginal revenue
AC	average cost
mpc	marginal prospensity to consume

EXAMPLE

Look at the specimen notes on Equilibrium in the Open Economy p.36. You may not fully understand them if you are at the beginning of your course, but consider how difficult it would be to represent the notes on that page:
—without the use of abbreviations.
—without the use of simple equations.

EXERCISE

(a) Look at the two sets of notes on p.37 about wage rates in particular occupations. These were made by two different students during the same lesson. What criticisms would you make of them as regards:
  (i) content?
 (ii) presentation?
(iii) organisation?
How much attention do you think was paid by each student to what was being said?
(b) How closely do your own notes resemble these notes? Be honest!
(c) Look in a textbook to try and find some more information about wage rates in particular occupations and rewrite the notes with supplementary material.

EXERCISE

A lot of advice has been given to you in this section. Bearing all this in mind, return to your own notes and spend some time improving them and making additions to them.

EQUILIBRIUM IN THE OPEN ECONOMY

The eqm. in the open economy is

$$Y = C + I + G + (x - m)$$

$(x-m)$ may be +ve or −ve, this is the B of P on current account

$$\text{Injections} = \text{Leakages}$$
$$I + G + X = M + S + T$$

It is tot. injections which <u>must</u> equal tot. leakages.

I does not have to equal S

G   "   "   "   "   "   T

M   "   "   "   "   "   X

The multiplier in the open economy

i) average propensity to import $= \dfrac{M}{Y}$ (APm)

ii) marginal   "   "   " $= \dfrac{\Delta M}{\Delta Y}$ (mPm)

If Y increases by 100 and M increases by 20 then   mPm = 0.2

The multiplier is: $\dfrac{1}{s + t + m}$

marginal propensity to save

marginal rate of tax

mPm

Wage rates in a JOB

("WHATS THAT"

Wage determined by Sup + Dem $

Elasticity of Labour $ ✪   Depends on M.R.P.

DEMAND OF LABOUR:
1) elasticity of demand for Product
2) Substitution ....
3) when wage Bill is a large Proportion of firm's Costs

$ Supply of Labour

① Standard of LIVING
② Power of Trade Unions
③ Mobility of Labour (CHANGE OF JOB)
④ Social Attitudes

WAGE RATES IN PARTICULAR OCCUPATIONS

The wage rate will be determined by the supply & demand for a particular type of labour. The demand for labour will depend on the M.R.P. The elasticity of demand for labour in any occupation will depend on:-

1. The elasticity of demand for the product
2. The possibility of substituting other factors
3. When the labour costs form a large or small proportion of total costs.

The supply of labour will depend on the following:-

1. Standard of living & the extent workers value leisure to income.
2. The power of trade unions & the power they have over recruitment.
3. The mobility of labour - changing jobs. Restrictions include family, training etc.
4. Social attitudes towards the nature of work.

C. WHAT TO MAKE NOTES ON

Central to your note-making should be a decision on what is important to your task. Further to this you will have to decide how much to write, which in turn will depend on your own strengths and weaknesses. If you can remember a fair amount of detail, you may not have to write so much, but be honest with yourself.

Writing too little can mean more work in the long run. The following guidelines should, however, help you to make your decision.

The Subject Matter

Different subjects will involve you in different requirements as far as notes are concerned but in Economics many topics follow a similar sort of pattern. Central to many topics is a theory and you should seek to use this theory in the description of a topic, in any analysis which you do and in any debate you are involved in. The diagram on p.39 represents the sort of pattern by which many topics can be represented. But also note the following broad principles:

DESCRIPTION

Generally description should form a relatively small part of your note-making. The study of any subject at A level requires much more than the ability merely to recount events and facts. Even so, you should be concerned with the description of any theories important to your line of study, as well as brief descriptions of any relevant economic events of the past or present.

APPLICATION AND ANALYSIS

Studying Economics requires you to understand and criticise quite complex analysis. You will need to use your knowledge of Economics in order to explain and interpret certain events and topics. No two economists will examine the same events in exactly the same way, because there are so many different perspectives which can be adopted. Do not worry, therefore, if your analysis is different from that of other people. All that is required of you is that you use your knowledge of Economics to the full. Remember that you will also need to examine any predictions which are a result of theories and analyses.

DEBATE

Economics is full of controversies and debates, and you should always try to reflect these in an objective way. Economists are famous for disagreeing with each other when talking about the implications and consequences of theories or contemporary events. This leads them to propose different policy options and argue about the possible results of these. Remembering that economists are human beings, you should always look for the influence of political ideology within the debate. This is particularly true when considering the management of the economy.

The Task

You will usually have a specific purpose for making notes and this should influence the type of notes you make. Relevance should be the key word. Irrelevant notes just take up time and can be very misleading, so think carefully about your task before and during your note-making to avoid this.

Some hints about making notes from different sources follow.

THEORY

1. What are the main assumptions, components, ideas and characteristics of the theory?
2. How, why and when was the theory developed?
3. What parallels or connections are there with other theories?
4. What is the meaning of specialised terms?

EVENTS OF THE PAST AND PRESENT

1. Is there a particular period of time important to this study?
2. Have events of the past had a significant influence on the work of economists?

APPLICATION

1. How can the theory be applied to the contemporary industrial economy, constituent parts of the economy or events of the past?
2. To what extent will external factors have an influence on the application?
3. To what extent will changes in institutions and circumstances have an influence on the application over time?

ANALYSIS

1. Is there a clear logical progression in the theory?
2. Is there a short run and a long run dimension?

PREDICTIONS

1. To what extent do predictions depend on the assumptions and the precise meaning of terms in the theory?
2. Is there a short run and a long run dimension?

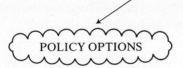

IMPLICATIONS AND CONSEQUENCES

1. What are the implications and consequences of the theory, application, analysis and predictions?
2. Have events of the past had an impact on the past and future?
3. Will any pattern which has emerged in the past repeat itself?

POLICY OPTIONS

1. Are there several policy options or just one or two?
2. Are the policy options clear?
3. Do the options complement or compete with each other?
4. What are the complete costs and benefits of the policies? Will there be 'knock-on' effects?

POLITICS AND IDEOLOGY

1. To what extent will the policy chosen depend on the political ideology of the policy maker?
2. Will policies change over the medium term (e.g. just before an election)?

RESULTS

1. If policies have been tried in the past, have they been a success or a failure?
2. Will the results of policies have an impact on analysis, application, predictions or even theory?
3. Can the results be clearly measured?

MAKING NOTES

SOURCE OF INFORMATION	SOME HINTS

LESSONS AND LECTURES	1. Determine your teacher's style:
	
	e.g. how does he/she emphasise key points
	     —on the board?
	     —by dictation?
	
	2. Listen out for key ideas. You should not try to note down everything that is said, but make a note of the overall structure of a topic. You can add details at a later stage.
	
	3. Develop a system for taking notes which will:
	    (a) speed up note-making;
	    (b) enable you to respond and contribute to the lesson.
	
	4. Pay particular attention to any recommended reading.
	
	5. Do not think of your lesson notes as finished products. They are really a starting-point. You should go away and add to them in your own time.
	
	6. If the teacher offers a summary at the end of a lesson, pay particular attention to it.
	
	7. Ask questions if you are unsure about anything.

TELEVISION AND RADIO PROGRAMMES	1. Decide whether this source is meant to be a major input of information or a supplement to existing knowledge. Either way, treat the session seriously. 2. If supplementary material is being provided, be sure to integrate this with your other notes. 3. Note in particular any applications and 'real world' examples which are provided. These can be useful to integrate into essays and other work.
BOOKS AND JOURNALS	1. Review the checklist at the end of Chapter 1. Be purposeful and active in your reading. 2. Make rough notes to begin with, then integrate these into your other notes. Review and reorganise all your notes from time to time. 3. Add examples and applications to your notes wherever they arise. These should illustrate your main points.

Adapted from table: *Taking Notes*, p.46, *The History Manual* (Framework Press, 1985), by J. A. Cloake, V. Crinnion and S. M. Harrison.

D.   ALTERNATIVE NOTE-MAKING METHODS

There are a number of ways to make good notes and you need to try them out in order to find out which suits you best. You will probably find that particular types of notes are best in particular circumstances and situations. Try to develop different note-making methods for different kinds of economic information. Making notes can become a pleasurable exercise when you alternate methods, but always bear in mind that your notes should be appropriate and accurate, and that the finished product should aid understanding and help with revision and memorisation.

Linear Notes

This is the most common method of note-making and for many students is the only form of notes used. Information, diagrams and ideas are kept in linear form on loose-leaf pages in a folder or binder.

Note-making is a continuous process and you will always be able to add something to your notes at a later stage. For this reason it is best not to fill up a sheet of paper with notes but to leave room either down the side of the page or at the bottom for additions.

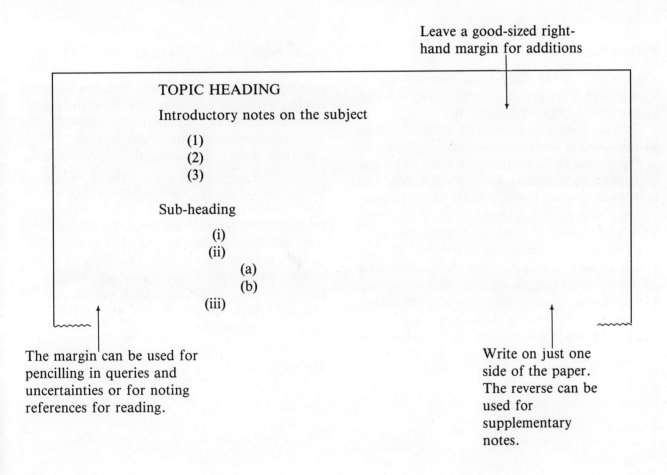

Leave a good-sized right-hand margin for additions

TOPIC HEADING

Introductory notes on the subject

(1)
(2)
(3)

Sub-heading

(i)
(ii)
(a)
(b)
(iii)

The margin can be used for pencilling in queries and uncertainties or for noting references for reading.

Write on just one side of the paper. The reverse can be used for supplementary notes.

Advantages of linear notes	Disadvantages of linear notes
1. They are familiar to the student and easy to write. 2. They can be clear and follow a logical progression. 3. Diagrams fit clearly into the scheme. 4. They allow for additional material to be added at a later date if space is left.	1. They can encourage copying from textbooks. It is easy to have a folder full of such notes without understanding any of them. 2. If space is not left, it can be difficult to add notes. 3. Linear notes can give you the impression of being exhaustive, comprehensive and complete. This will rarely be the case. 4. Linear notes make it difficult to show complex links and multi-dimensional concepts. 5. It is often difficult to form an image of linear notes in your mind. This may hamper revision.

Pattern Notes

Pattern notes avoid many of the disadvantages of linear notes. They provide a flexible way in which to present economic information.

They are particularly useful when there is a flow of information containing interrelationships, but are less useful if the written work needs to be supplemented by diagrams, so find out before you start making notes if this is likely to be the case.

The idea of pattern notes is to begin at the centre of a clean sheet of paper and write down the central idea or main heading. You should then use this as a base to branch out from, firstly with more important ideas and subsequently with less important ideas and concepts. Use key words rather than sentences, so that the pattern does not get congested. Strong links can be shown with bold connections, whereas less important or more tentative links or interrelationships can be shown with dotted lines. The links between concepts will thus be clearly recognised. Generally, the nearer points are to the centre of the pattern and the bolder the connection, the more important they are.

Pattern notes can significantly help recall. Most people find it easier to store a visual picture of subject matter in their minds than reams of linear notes which can appear to be all the same. The structure of any pattern should not be too cluttered and there should be space left so that additional notes can be included. It can be a lot of fun making pattern notes especially if you are able to incorporate small sketches. Each pattern will be unique, which in turn helps you recall and memorise information.

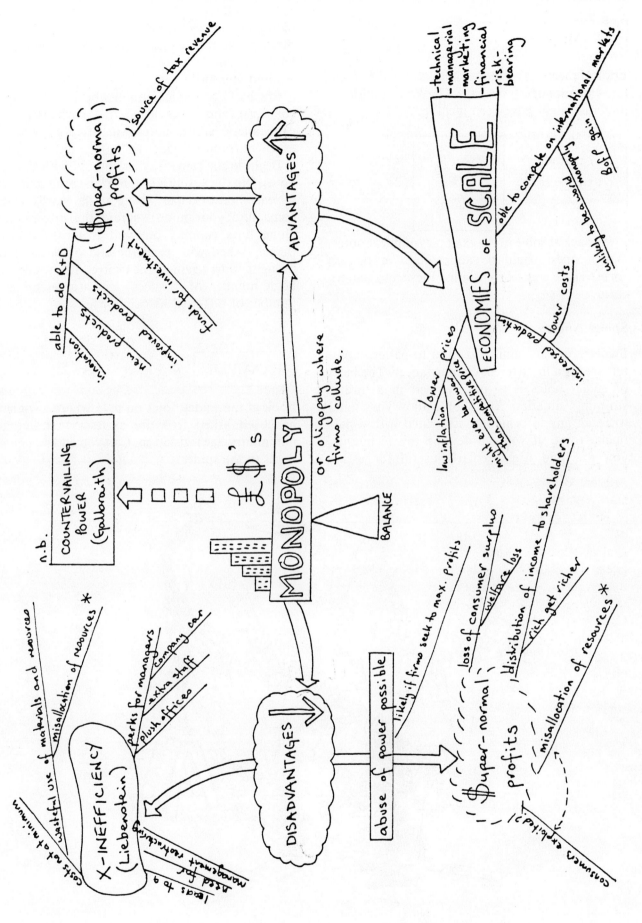

EXAMPLE

Look at the notes on the advantages and disadvantages of monopoly on page 43. What additional material might have been included?

EXERCISE

Look back at some of the examples of linear notes. Which ones would be appropriate in pattern form? Have a go at translating these into pattern form.

Spider Notes

Spider notes are similar in form to pattern notes but are used in different circumstances. The basis of spider notes is to put yourself in a 'brainstorming' situation. You should allow your mind to recall any information associated with a particular topic. If you can develop this technique, you will find it particularly useful for essay-planning and revision exercises. The process can often boost your confidence, since you will probably remember more information than you had realised you knew.

Much of Economics is about applying economic concepts and knowledge to particular circumstances; spider notes will often provide an excellent frame on which to 'hang' your thoughts.

Begin in the same way as you did with pattern notes. Put the key idea or question at the centre of a clean sheet of paper. Using all the words which come into your mind, 'spray' the information along lines running outward from the central theme. When you reach the end of one line of thought, start again at the centre. The result will be a number of 'spiders' legs' representing a number of different associations.

EXAMPLE

Look at the spider notes on p.45 where a student has been asked to write an essay relating to minimum wage legislation. Can you add any more 'legs' to the spider?

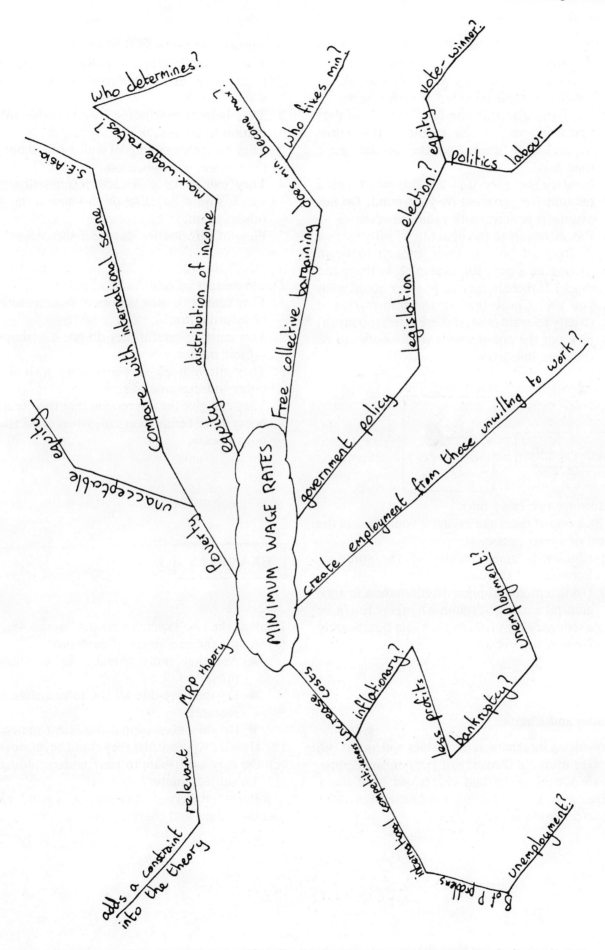

When you have finished the spider, look at the pattern and survey the words, connections and sequences in the following way (you may like to look at the example provided at each stage):

(a) Pay particular attention to repetitions of particular words. In the example, the words 'equity' and 'unemployment' appear more than once.

(b) Note the sequence of ideas. This may reveal a relationship perceived by your mind. Do not assume it is necessarily valid, however.

(c) Pay attention to the quantity of information in front of you. Is there enough to begin writing an essay, for example? Is there too much? If there is, then be selective about what you use. Check that all the information is strictly relevant, and, if there is still too much, pick out the points which you consider to be the most important.

EXERCISE

Below are two essay titles.

Pick one of them and organise your ideas in the form of spider notes:

(a) 'Choice is at the centre of the study of Economics.' Discuss.

(b) Using a model of price determination in agricultural markets, explain why there might be a tendency for prices to fluctuate significantly from year to year.

Tables and Charts

Organising information into tables and charts can be very useful in the study of Economics. Appropriate use of tables and charts can have many advantages, but they should not be used when a lot of information is involved.

Advantages of tables and charts:

1. They show interrelationships between concepts, facts and arguments in an analytical way.

2. They help memorisation by presenting information in an unique way.

3. They have a visual impact which stimulates the note-maker's imagination.

4. They can make clear any interrelationships which would be difficult to show using any other system.

5. Flow of information can be demonstrated.

Disadvantages of tables and charts:

1. They cannot be used to present large quantities of information.

2. You must be careful they do not oversimplify subject matter.

3. They often need supplementing with linear notes and explanations.

4. They can give the impression that the situation being described is clear-cut, when often this is not the case.

EXAMPLES

Look at the two examples on p.47 and p.48.

(a) Assess the usefulness of each one:
  ● Are they more useful than continuous prose?
  ● Do they provide all the information you require?
  ● Do they need supporting linear material?

(b) How do you consider they could be improved?

(c) Do they contribute to your understanding of the subject matter?

Remember to keep these points in mind when you use tables and charts.

COMPETITION POLICY (U.K.)

THE MACHINERY OF STATE CONTROL

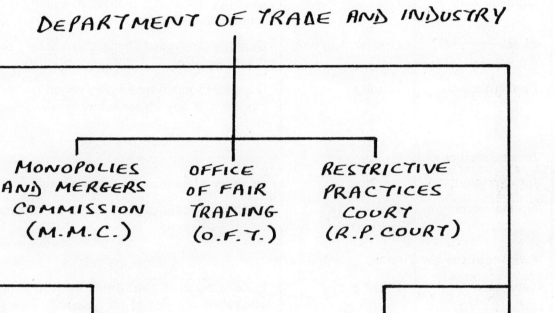

DEPARTMENT OF TRADE AND INDUSTRY

MONOPOLIES AND MERGERS COMMISSION (M.M.C.)

OFFICE OF FAIR TRADING (O.F.T.)

RESTRICTIVE PRACTICES COURT (R.P. COURT)

NATIONAL CONSUMER COUNCIL

CONSUMER PROTECTION ADVISORY COMMITTEE

LOCAL AUTHORITIES (e.g. TRADING STANDARDS DEPT.)

CITIZENS' ADVICE BUREAUX (C.A.B.)

ELASTICITY OF DEMAND

Terminology	Numerical measure	Description
Price elasticity		
Perfectly inelastic	Zero	Quantity demanded does not change as price changes.
Inelastic	Greater than zero, less than one.	Quantity demanded changes by a smaller percentage than does price.
Unit elasticity	One	Quantity demanded changes by exactly the same percentage as does price.
Elastic	Greater than one	Quantity demanded changes by a larger percentage than does price.
Perfectly elastic	Infinity	Buyers will purchase all they can at one price but will buy none at any higher price.
Income elasticity		
Inferior good	Negative	Quantity demanded decreases as income increases.
Normal good	Positive	Quantity demanded increases as income increases.
Cross-elasticity		
Substitute	Positive	Price increase of a substitute leads to an increase in quantity demanded of this good.
Complement	Negative	Price increase of a complement leads to a decrease in quantity demanded of this good.

EXERCISES

(a) Draw a chart/diagram to represent the circular flow of income in an open economy with a government sector. Remember to show all injections (investment, government spending and exports) and all leakages (saving, taxation and imports). Saving and investment will represent the monetary sector and imports and exports the international sector.

(b) Copy and complete the table on the next page, which is designed to show the advantages and disadvantages of nationalisation and privatisation and any links between the arguments.

Nationalisation		Privatisation	
Advantages	Disadvantages	Advantages	Disadvantages

Which columns have points in common?

Card Indexes

Card indexes have two main uses, firstly as a convenient method of keeping a note of important terminology and concepts and secondly as final revision notes.

IMPORTANT TERMINOLOGY AND CONCEPTS

Information about particular or unfamiliar economic terms and concepts can easily be kept in a card index consisting of a number of postcard-sized entries in alphabetical order. These can easily be referred to when needed. Cards are very cheap and, depending on number, can be kept together with a bulldog clip or an elastic band, or, where there is a large number of cards, in a proper index box (available from stationers) or in a shoe box.

FINAL REVISION NOTES

Final revision notes should be brief, and contain only the important points about any topic, which should 'spark off' related points and other knowledge which you have. These can easily be used for quick reference. Moreover, they are easily carried and, if you take them around with you, there will often be opportunities to glance at them (on the bus for example). As with linear notes, it is useful to leave space on the cards for additional material.

E. SUMMARY

METHOD	APPROPRIATE ACTIVITY	ADVANTAGES	DISADVANTAGES
LINEAR	1. Descriptions 2. Notes integrated with technical diagrams 3. Essay drafts 4. Lesson notes	1. Easy to make 2. A lot of detail can be included 3. Vocabulary and style can be developed	1. May discourage analysis 2. Can encourage copying 3. Key ideas can easily be lost
PATTERN	1. Analysis of topics 2. Lesson notes	1. Memorable 2. Interesting and fun 3. Analytical 4. Concise 5. Visual impact	1. Impossible to incorporate diagrams 2. Unfamiliar at first 3. Not much room for detail
SPIDER	1. Essay-planning 2. Brain-storming 3. Revision and recall	1. Enables logical progression 2. Helps flow of information 3. Provides reassurance over quantity of information	1. Cannot provide a lot of detail 2. Easy to get 'side-tracked'
TABLES AND CHARTS	1. Diagrams of institutional arrangements 2. Lists of alternative and complementary arguments 3. Statistical information	1. Can show complex interrelationships 2. Visual impact helps revision	1. Danger of over-simplification 2. Cannot contain large quantities of information
CARD INDEXES	1. Lists of terminology and concepts 2. Revision aids	1. Easily arranged 2. Quick access 3. Can contain further references 4. Portable	1. Only carry a small amount of information

Adapted from table 'A Summary of Methods and Uses', p.64, *The History Manual* (Framework Press, 1985) by J. A. Cloake, V. Crinnion and S. M. Harrison

F. CHECKLIST √ √ √ √ √ √ √ √ √ √ √

1	Try to experiment (more than once) with each of the different note-making methods.
2	Come to a decision as to which method suits you best. Remember that it is quite valid to use different note-making methods in different situations.
3	Are you using your notes to develop your understanding as well as recording information from lessons and books?.
4	Are you ensuring that diagrams are accurate?
5	Learn to distinguish the difference between economic analysis and interpretation, and mere description.
6	Practise making notes from sources where you will need to distil large amounts of information into manageable essentials.
7	Ensure that you review and revise your notes periodically as your knowledge and understanding increases.

Note-making in bed,
Comfortable—but is it efficient?

G. END OF CHAPTER EXERCISE

Employing the note-making skills developed in this chapter, use the following passage to try out the various methods of note-making suggested:

POLICY IMPLICATIONS FOR THE INFORMATION TECHNOLOGY AGE:
A PERSONAL ANALYSIS by Richard Welford

If employment is to grow and not decline in the future, as technology continues to advance, then there are implications for the organisational and institutional structure of the economy. There are no simple policy solutions. Nevertheless, there does seem to be some scope for demand reflationary policies when coupled with policies aimed more at a restructuring of parts of the economy and of some of the institutions which have failed to react to the changes which have occurred since 1980.

There are implications for the firm, for the organisation of work and for education and training. These are dealt with in turn.

Within the firm

Technology and information technology have increased the flexibility of the firm. The adoption of computer-aided design, for example, allows firms to develop and change products much more frequently in response to changing consumer tastes. It also enables firms to handle larger amounts of data at minimal cost. This means more effective stock control for example and a resultant cost-saving in the requirement to hold fewer inventories. Information technology in particular gives the firm more scope for decentralised decision-making and creates less of a need for hierarchical professional management structures.

The 'Alvey' programme, launched in 1983, has encouraged the adoption of new technology in firms and has also encouraged many partnerships between industry and higher education. In many instances this has been taken up, but more is yet required and there is a need for further government support, especially in the areas of research and development. Between 1979 and 1988 the government spent less on civil research and development as a percentage of gross national product, than Japan, Germany, Sweden or Switzerland.

The organisation of work

Even more than ever, there is a need for flexibility in the workplace. This requires workers as well as managers to have multiple skills and undergo retraining, including the development of computer literacy. Institutional barriers need removing to allow various forms of more flexible working. Not only would this include flexible hours, but also early retirement, work-sharing, part-time working and career breaks.

From a policy perspective, there is a need for an increased supply of very highly-qualified people in computer-related technologies. We also need a more generally-educated workforce with adaptability, which would include some basic computer literacy training for everybody.

. . . continued

Systems of consultation between workers and management also need to be changed with the new technology to create a more participative workforce.

Implications for education and training

Many of the statistics available on the unemployed and job vacancies suggest that there is a significant mismatch between the two. We now have a shortage of skilled people, the result being that firms are less productive.

Thus, there is a need to improve both the quality and quantity of education, training and retraining. In the U.K. there has been an expression of technologically-biased education and training, largely via the support of the Manpower Services Commission and their Youth Training Scheme (YTS) and Technical and Vocational Education Initiative (TVEI).

But a substantial problem in higher-level education has been the fact that the best educators have also been attracted away from education in the U.K. either by industry or by significantly higher salaries overseas. There is need to expand higher education, especially to take up non-traditional entry students, if we are to have enough highly-educated people to support growing industries. To this end, education must be financed as if it were an investment good, capable of high returns, rather than a consumption good.

Conclusions

Just as there is no single policy aimed at integrating technology into the economy, there cannot be a single conclusion about what mix of policies is optimal. It all rather depends on one's perspectives and priorities. Nevertheless, if we examine the success of the Japanese economy, we see it is based on two things: firstly, a rapid diffusion of technology and secondly a considerable amount of targeted government support and innovation. If the U.K. is to benefit from the I.T. revolution, there seems to be a need for considerable support and investment by the government, not only in industry, but also in the institutional structure of the economy.

ESSAY-WRITING

		Page
A.	WHY WRITE ESSAYS?	56
B.	QUESTION ANALYSIS	57
	Question Analysis by Part	58
	Understanding the Question	59
	Information Content	60
C.	APPROACHES TO ESSAY-WRITING	61
D.	PLANNING YOUR ESSAY	63
	Collecting Material and Selecting Information	63
	Stage 1: Collecting the Material	63
	Stage 2: Selecting the Information	65
	The Essay Plan	65
E.	DRAFTING, RE-DRAFTING AND EDITING THE ESSAY	70
	Drafting and Re-drafting	70
	Editing	72
F.	IMPORTANT ASPECTS OF THE ESSAY	73
	The Introduction	73
	The Structure of the Essay	76
	Relevance	76
	Logical Argument	77
	Style and Presentation	80
	The Conclusion	82
G.	ASSESSMENT AND FOLLOW-UP	84
	Assessment by the Marker	84
	Self-Assessment	86
	Discussion with Other Students	86
	The Essay-Writing Process	87
H.	CHECKLIST	88

A. WHY WRITE ESSAYS?

Much of your important writing will be in the form of essays. You are required to do much of your thinking through writing. It will involve you in a commitment of time, energy and mental effort. You will eventually become more proficient in such skills as question analysis, interpreting topics, handling research and resources, and mastering the technical language sometimes associated with Economics. But the first struggle will involve you in shaping your thoughts into the written word and connecting those thoughts into a coherent and logical argument.

Essays are used to assess your performance and ultimately to test your knowledge and understanding of Economics in the examination. But they should be seen in the first instance as an integral part of your own studies, developing your thinking in new fields for new purposes.

Essays are designed so that you are able to demonstrate certain skills. These can be divided into four areas:

(a) A knowledge and understanding of factual material.

(b) An ability to draw conclusions from information of various types.

(c) An ability to evaluate differing opinions, arguments and lines of thought in a positive, unbiased way.

(d) An ability to organise relevant knowledge in an analysis of questions of Economics.

Marks will generally be awarded in line with these skills according to how proficiently they are tackled. In every essay there will be a solid block of factual information, but that on its own is insufficient to gain a good mark. Most marks are awarded for demonstrating more sophisticated skills. These include interpretation, analysis and judgement.

What NOT to do when writing essays

There are many misleading comments made about essay writing, usually by people who do not know any better. Here is a list of things to avoid:

● Do not stay up all night to write an essay. You will not make a good job of writing it when you are tired and you will probably mess up the following day's studies as well.

● Do not just waffle on. Your essay must be well argued and well reasoned. Irrelevant material will not gain you a good mark—or indeed any marks.

● There is no specific skill required for writing an essay which some people have and others do not. There are strategies for approaching the writing of an essay which we will concentrate on this chapter, but no one set of skills will guarantee success, just as there is no perfect essay. You need to develop, practise and master the skills required to enable you to write a good Economics essay.

B. QUESTION ANALYSIS

Understanding what a question is asking of you will help you to answer it. Thus, this section looks at the essay question and examines how you should work out exactly what it means and what emphasis you are being asked to place on various aspects of it.

Every question will require you to apply your understanding of Economics to specific situations and to select, organise and structure relevant information in order to answer the question. Most of the marks in an essay will be awarded for demonstrating that you can apply your skills to answering the question as set. For this reason the questions you are asked will test not only your memory, but a range of other skills associated with your study of Economics.

Essay questions will be worded with care. Your teacher or the examiner will have an idea of what is expected in the answer. Although this does not mean that there is only one way to write the essay, it does mean that there are limits to the way it should be handled. You should, at the outset, take time to analyse what is being asked and to note any particular emphasis given by the wording of the question. You must decide if there are any key concepts being asked for. Following the initial question analysis it will be necessary to think about relevant materials to be used in your writing.

EXAMPLE

Look at the following essay question:

Compare and contrast the free-enterprise system with the centrally-planned system for allocating scarce resources.

Now consider the following questions based on what has been said above:
(a) What specific topic are you being asked to examine?
(b) What limits have been imposed on what you should cover?
(c) Is there any particular emphasis in the wording?
(d) What key concepts have been mentioned?
(e) What direction, relating to your style of answer, is being asked for (e.g. are you being asked to discuss, critically appraise, compare, contrast, etc.)?

Answers:

(a) An examination of the free-enterprise system, based on the price mechanism, i.e. the interaction of supply and demand, is required first of all. Following this, contrast should be drawn with the centrally-planned system, where a powerful authority makes the decisions about what to produce, how to produce and how to distribute goods and services.
(b) Only the free-enterprise system and the centrally-planned system should be covered. It may be worthwhile mentioning that these two extremes are not used in practice, but that most countries operate along a spectrum of 'mixed economies'. Other forms of economic system are not required, however.
(c) 'Compare and contrast' seems important. The request is that the two systems are seen side by side and various aspects compared with each other. The implication is not that there should be half an essay on one system and half on the other.
(d) The key concepts mentioned are centrally-planned system, free-enterprise system and scarce resources. You will need to spell out what each of these means.
(e) 'Compare and contrast' (see item (c)).

Have a look at the following essay titles and ask yourself the same questions:

(i) *To what extent can orthodox national income accounting methods be employed as a useful indicator of welfare between countries?*
(ii) *'The privatisation of large, previously publicly owned corporations makes them more efficient and gives the public a chance to become shareholders in important national enterprises.' Discuss this view applied to the privatisation of one national corporation of which you have knowledge.*
(iii) *How are wages determined? How do you therefore account for the differences in wages paid to doctors, teachers and road-sweepers?*
(iv) *'The benefits of reducing inflation below 10% have not been worth the costs imposed on the unemployed of attaining that result.' Discuss.*
(v) *Critically appraise the effects of an increase in the exchange rate on the domestic economy.*

Question Analysis by Part

Having gained an overview of what the question is asking, you can now take a more detailed look at the question by taking it apart and examining its elements.

It is possible to divide a question up into three parts:
1. The instruction
2. The main topic
3. The key factor or key words.

EXAMPLE

Consider the following question:

> *To what extent is the theory of perfect competition useful to the economist?*

1. The instruction or the part of the question telling you what to do is contained in the phrase: *'To what extent'*.
2. The topic which you are requested to consider is the *theory of perfect competition*.
3. The key factor revolves around the consideration of whether the theory is *of use to the economist*.

Thus, your answer should outline the theory of perfect competition and comment on how useful it is to the economist in particular. You will realise once you have studied the topic that the theory of perfect competition can be criticised for being theoretical and not reflecting the real world. But it does nevertheless act as a benchmark against which we can examine other market structures. This can be mentioned in your analysis of the *extent* of its usefulness.

EXAMPLE

By using a different symbol or colour to identify each part of the question, divide up the following essay questions into the three parts outlined above:
(i) *Discuss the contention that the government should seek to cure unemployment by means of micro-economic rather than macro-economic policies.*
(ii) *Critically appraise the policy of cutting social security benefits as a means of reducing unemployment.*
(iii) *Assess the impact of the micro-electronic revolution on the U.K.'s growth prospects into the next century.*

QUESTIONS WITH MORE THAN ONE PART

Often essay questions will be asked in two (or occasionally more) parts. The parts will normally be related to each other. A common technique is to ask you to outline some economic theory in the first part of a question and then to use that theory in the second part. The question can nevertheless be broken down into parts.

EXAMPLE

Consider the following question:

> *Outline a theory of oligopoly with which you are familiar. To what extent is this theory capable of explaining the sort of price leadership often reflected in the petrol retailing sector?*

Let us examine the question one half at a time:
In the first half of the question, the *instruction* is to 'outline'. The *main topic* is a theory of oligopoly, but note that it does not specify any particular one. That choice is up to you, but you will gain more marks if you chose a theory which can subsequently be used in the second half of the question.

The second half of the question has the *instruction*: 'To what extent'. The *main topics* are the sort of price leadership reflected in the petrol industry (which you will need to explain) and the theory of oligopoly. The *key phrase* is 'capable of explaining'.

EXERCISE

Do the same type of analysis with the following questions:

(i) *Outline the concept of the price mechanism. Why is it necessary for the government to interfere in this mechanism occasionally?*

(ii) *Discuss the efficiency of quotas as a method of reducing farm surpluses.*

(iii) *'If unions succeed in raising real wages, this will lead to less employment and ultimately a smaller total of wages.' Evaluate this statement.*

(iv) *What factors may limit the efficacy of variations in interest rates as a weapon of policy?*

PARAPHRASING THE QUESTION

Having analysed the parts of a question, you should rephrase the question using your own words, concentrating on the key factor or words. This will help your understanding of the question.

EXAMPLE

Using the first two questions above, we can paraphrase them in the following way:

(i) After explaining the price mechanism, *state the necessity* for the government to interfere with it.

(ii) *Focus on the efficiency* of quotas for the reduction of farm surpluses.

Notice that in the paraphrase the key factor appears as the central theme of the question. This is usually situated at the beginning (or the start of the appropriate half) of the question. It is given its proper attention by placing it first.

EXERCISE

Paraphrase questions (iii) and (iv) above, remembering that they key factor or words should appear first.

How will this help?

(a) The key factor or words are even more important that the main topic.

(b) Paraphrasing brings the key factor of the question to the surface and forces you to concentrate on it.

(c) Paraphrasing will help you stick to relevant aspects of the question.

(d) By paraphrasing you will be able to assess how well you understand and can answer the question.

Understanding the Question

In order to answer a question fully you must understand the full implications of the question. You need to look at what might be hidden in the question. Questions often imply things which are not actually made explicit. In other words the question may suggest something indirectly.

EXAMPLE

Consider the following essay question:

Discuss the contention that unemployment can be significantly reduced by reducing unemployment benefit.

Some economists have indeed argued that this is the case. But what is the hidden implication in the question? Simply that a significant number of unemployed people are not unemployed because they cannot find jobs, but because, given the present levels of benefit, it is not worth their while working. In your answer you would be required to say whether this appears to be true on a significant scale. Where is the evidence to support or refute this?

Obviously, to recognise implications in questions you need some knowledge of the topic. This can be achieved in your reading. You should familiarise yourself with the topic and search for the implications of a question. In other words you must start to apply your broad knowledge to the specific question.

EXERCISE

Below are three essay questions. Can you detect any implications which would need to be carefully considered in each one?

(i) *'The costs of unemployment do not only include the lost production associated with unemployed resources and the money which has to be spent on unemployment benefits but also significant social costs.'* Discuss.

(ii) *'Privatisation represents merely a change in the ownership of previously state-owned monopolies. Changes in profitability will therefore only be the result of a strengthening of monopoly power.'* Comment on this view in the light of the privatisation programme of the 1980s.

(iii) *Discuss the contention that unemployment statistics for women are a gross underestimate of the real figures because many women who would like to work full-time can only get part-time jobs.*

Information Content

Questions can often include a lot of information within them. These questions may be off-putting at first because they are likely to be longer, but often you can use the additional information to your advantage.

Consider the following questions:
(i) *Have the policies of privatisation introduced in the 1980s proved to be a success?*
(ii) *The government is considering whether to support the construction of a new motorway running directly from London to the North-East. Outline all the costs and benefits, both financial and non-financial, that this would imply. What would you consider to be the likely impact on the depressed North-East if this were to go ahead?*

The two questions have a very different information content. The second question may look daunting at first, but let us examine how much help you are given in the question.

Question (i)

You are asked to assess the success of the privatisation policies of the 1980s. Obviously you need to outline those policies and then go on to discuss their success. But how are we defining success? There are many different measures of success and the question does not help you here. You would need to spend time discussing just what successful means in terms of privatisation. Clearly, however you define success there will be those who disagree and you will need to support your definition in order to get a good mark.

We can now see that in fact the question is rather difficult. You are given very little help with what to write in your answer.

Question (ii)

This question is brim-full of information. Let us list the help you are given:

● The question relates specifically to the construction of a motorway running from London to the North-East.
● You are asked to outline the costs and benefits of its construction, and helpfully reminded that these will be both financial (e.g. the amount of money which will be spent on the construction) and non-financial (e.g. the loss of agricultural land and increase in pollution).
● You are subsequently asked to comment on the likely impact on the North-East and you are reminded that the North-East is a depressed area.

A lot of information is being given to you.

Long questions are often avoided by students, particularly if they begin with the instruction 'Discuss'. It is natural that we should all prefer straightforward wording and form. However, some of the most complex-looking questions can be the most unthreatening and helpful titles.

Remember:
(a) Complex questions can be simple tasks in disguise.
(b) The more information in the question, the more you will be aware of its demands.
(c) Extra information in the question will help you focus on the most relevant aspects.
(d) Information can provide you with a structure for your answer.
(e) You only need more patience to unravel the wording of a long question, not more ability.

EXERCISE

Assess the information content in the following essay titles:
(i) *Discuss the effectiveness of British merger policy. To what extent is it only capable of dealing with horizontal merger activity?*
(ii) *The high inflation and high unemployment associated with the 1970s was argued by many to imply the end of the Phillips curve relationship. With reference to the expectations-augmented Phillips curve, discuss whether or not this is the case.*
(iii) *Outline the reasons for the apparent inverse relationship between interest rates and the price of government bonds.*
(iv) *The pharmaceutical industry in the U.K. is characterised by a few large firms spending large sums of money on advertising research and development. Comment on whether such expenditure is to be expected in this type of market structure.*

C. APPROACHES TO ESSAY-WRITING

The essay is a vital part of your study of Economics. It is the vehicle through which you must demonstrate your abilities. Essays are central to your work throughout the course and in the examination itself.

The table on p.62 shows three approaches to the essay-writing problem. These approaches are not mutually exclusive and indeed you are likely to change your approach as you proceed with your studies.

TYPE	METHOD	REASONS FOR METHOD	ADVANTAGES OF METHOD	DISADVANTAGES OF METHOD
'Sit down and do it'	Writes essay straight off, without planning or preparing from notes, old essays, text books, memory. 'that will do.' 'I must get it done for tomorrow.'	1. Laziness. 2. Disorganisation. 3. Incompetence. 4. Carelessness/ casualness. 5. Lack of time. 6. Brilliance.	1. Quick. 2. Meets deadlines. 3. Leaves time for football, discos, T.V.	1. Inadequate time for thinking. 2. Rough or poor appearance. 3. Imperfect espression of ideas. 4. Irrelevance. 5. Disjointed.
'Planning'	Plans essay and resources to be used, then writes up.	1. Has read 'The Economics Manual'. 2. Good organisation of time. 3. Efficient.	1. Efficient use of time. 2. Considered, relevant essay. 3. Logical arrangement of ideas and materials. 4. Excellent preparation for examinations.	
'In rough, then in neat'	Writes out whole essay in rough form, copies up into a neat version.	1. Misguided concern for appearance above relevance, argument and general content. 2. Masochism. 3. Concern to produce a definitive essay; a contribution to the wisdom of the ages.	1. Neat final essay. 2. Well-constructed relevant essay? 3. Better than those following the 'sit down and do it' approach.	1. Uses vast amounts of time—very slow. 2. Essays can become shorter in length, therefore inadequate treatment of question. 3. Tendency to copy out plans in fuller form during exams.

Table: 'Approaches to Essay Writing, adapted from p.84, *The History Manual* (Framework Press, 1985) by J. A. Cloake, V. Crinnion and S. M. Harrison

It is important that your essay is presented well. It should be neat and legible. Examiners will not give you the benefit of the doubt if it is unreadable.

Remember that you will not be expected to produce excellent essays at the beginning of your studies. There is a skill in essay-writing which needs to be developed and you should improve with practice. Even if on one or two occasions your essay turns out to be poor, you will nevertheless have learned something from it.

As important as the final essay itself is the process by which it was achieved.

The note-making and reading which will necessarily have gone into a good essay will be of benefit in other areas. You should not see the writing of the essay as an isolated event.

The implication of the table is that in the early stages of essay-writing a process of drafting, redrafting and editing may be a good way to proceed. However, with practice you should aim to cut out the redrafting. If you aim for good planning, the time-consuming task of redrafting and editing will become less necessary. Remember that in the final examination you will only have time to plan and write your essay.

As you progress and become more proficient, you should concentrate more on the planning of your essay than on constant revision of it. You will find this gets easier as you become more confident about essay-writing and about Economics.

Section G looks at what follow-up should be done after you have received your marked essay. Teachers' comments will be very important and you should read them and respond to them. If you have got a low mark and cannot understand why it is so low, then consult your teacher. In this way you will be able to learn from your mistakes.

D.   PLANNING YOUR ESSAY

Once you have selected a question, there are two tasks which you ought to do next. Firstly, where this is possible (that is to say when the essay is not being written in examination conditions), you should collect materials, and secondly, you should sketch out an essay plan.

Collecting material and selecting information

STAGE 1: COLLECTING THE MATERIAL

Your material will come from a variety of sources:

- Books
- Articles
- Reports
- Other documents
- Lesson/lecture notes
- Personal observations
- Other people's observations
- Television and radio programmes

Do not forget to record the sources of your ideas. These should be presented in a bibliography (a list of sources) at the end of your essay. As far as possible, note the following information:

—author
—title
—publisher or source
—date of publication
—chapter and page numbers

Before plunging into the selection, you should assess just what is available by surveying the material. The selection of your material should be directed by the essay question. Always bear this in mind so as to avoid collecting too much information. Make use of course reading lists and look in the indexes of books which you think might help. Also look at subject catalogues in libraries and consult your teacher on what he/she considers to be the best sources of reference.

Look at the material which you have found and decide on its relevance to the specific question. Remember to ask yourself questions and work out possible answers before turning to the books. Do not only read what you agree with, as this may just be confirming your own prejudices. Search for material which has a contradictory viewpoint. Most arguments in Economics have at least two viewpoints and you must be aware of these disagreements and conflicts and be able to present them in a balanced way.

Your own first-hand observations can be useful. But if you are going to make comments based on your own observations, make sure you really can back them up and justify them. Throwaway statements which are unsubstantiated and therefore weak will not gain you marks.

Think and do all your preliminary work first.

If you have asked yourself questions in order to guide the amount of material you collect, you should not have an unmanageable amount. Nevertheless, it will be necessary to sift through the material, cutting out that which in retrospect is not relevant and that which is essentially saying the same as other sources.

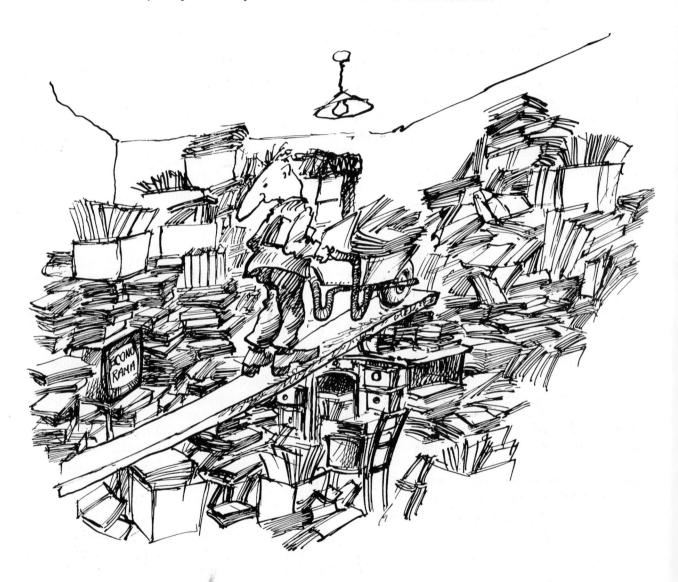

Do not be tempted to try to show how much you have done, i.e. to use it all. Do not consider it a waste of time collecting material you do not think you will use. Add it to your notes, where it may be useful at a later stage.

The process of selecting and discarding material should be carried out by reconsidering the essay title in conjunction with writing an essay plan.

EXERCISE

Go back through the essay titles given in this chapter and make lists of sources of material which you might consider using in order to produce answers.

STAGE 2: SELECTING THE INFORMATION

When writing your essay, it is likely that you will have more material than is necessary. You must select the material which best fits the essay question. It is surprising how many essays are spoiled because students include too much information, much of it irrelevant. Piling up information for the sake of it often means that the essay is repetitive.

The Essay Plan

There are a number of very important reasons why it is advisable to make an outline plan before writing up your essay:

- Your argument is tested in the plan to see if it is convincing. You discover in advance whether you have the information to answer the question.
- All your resources are brought together in the plan.
- It makes a well-structured essay far more likely.
- It is easier for you to organise your thoughts when you are writing the essay. You can move from point to point in a systematic and logical way.
- The plan helps to prevent mistakes, waffle, inaccuracy and repetition.

- It saves time in the long run.
- If you are used to planning, you will produce a more relevant and direct answer in examinations.

Look over the material you have selected. Decide on what you consider to be the main points and think about how these can be collected together to lead to a conclusion.

The broad structure of the essay should be:

—Introduction
—Main body
—Conclusion

If you are given a word limit, say 1,000 words, you might split this up as follows:

—Introduction   125 words or less
—Main body   600–700 words
—Conclusion   200–250 words

This will help you keep the right proportions. Within the main body of the essay you will now further need to plan what you are going to write.

Your plan should reflect a logical approach. Try to arrange your material so as to flow from one point to another, rather than jumping disjointedly from one point to another. Draw attention to the interrelationships within the points. If one argument is directly opposed to another one, make this clear.

Let us now examine some plans and see how they can help.

EXAMPLE

Consider the following essay title:

> *The last decade has seen a movement of workers from the North of the country to the South. Discuss the possible reasons for this and the consequences for the respective halves of the country.*

Two essay plans are presented in response to this question:

<u>Essay</u>   ①

The last decade has seen a movement of workers from the North of the country to the South. <u>Discuss</u> the possible <u>reasons</u> for this and the <u>consequences</u> for the respective halves of the country.

<u>Introduction</u>

Migration   North – South divide   N ↑ ↓ S

<u>Reasons</u>

Jobs + higher wages.
Decline of N. Industry ← Shipbuilding Textiles
New industry in South → (microelectronics) services.

Regional policy

Makes it worse

<u>Consequences</u> :

North run down ←
South booms ←

N. Unemployment
N. needs help from govt.
Lack of skilled workers in N
   because they've all gone south
   — makes situation worse

House prices !

International market – Dover – EEC

n.b. incentives
Popn of N. elderly / retired etc.

<u>Conclusions</u>

ESSAY PLAN ②

SOUTH   NORTH

REASONS

1. Growth in jobs, partic. in "new industries" and services.

2. But note "misinformation" about availability of jobs. There is still unemployment in South (James, ch. 2).

3. Growth in international market.

4. Demand for labour => higher wages.

1. Decline in traditional industries (e.g textiles, shipbuilding,) => loss of jobs. (See Smith pp. 69-74).

2. Experiences of long-term unemployed and high youth unemployment. (James ch.2)

3. Relatively low wages even when people are in work.

CONSEQUENCES

1. South continues to expand: not constrained by lack of skilled workers.

2. But growth of unemployment amongst unskilled.

3. Demand for houses => property prices rise and increases cost of living (diagram?).

4. Growing inequalities between N and S.

1. Lack of skilled workers: hinders new development: vicious circle.

2. N. gets further run down as people move out.

3. Needs increasing govt. spending on social benefits, incentives to new firms, etc. (regional policy see Smith pp 77-87).

4. Popn. declining in N.

CONCLUSION
1. Need for regional policy directed at N.
2. Otherwise vicious circle continues

EXERCISE

Look at each plan in turn. Which one more closely resembles your plans?

List the advantages and disadvantages of each plan.

Things to note from the example plans:

(a) Plan 1 is not at all clear. Certain points are made which do not appear to fall under appropriate section headlines. This student did not have all his/her attention on the task in hand.

(b) Neither plan offers us a logical progression. It is not clear which point should follow which.

(c) There are no references to readings or other source materials in plan 1, and in plan 2 only two sources are mentioned.

(d) In both plans there appears to be repetition of points.

(c) Both plans use the phrase 'run down'—but what exactly does this mean?

EXERCISE

Do some more reading around this subject and present the plan which you think is most appropriate to the task of answering the question. The following table will help you:

HOW TO PLAN FOR ESSAYS	REASONS
1. Use plenty of space.	It will be easier to read and follow when writing.
2. Plan in pencil with a rubber.	It will allow you to re-arrange and correct information.
3. Leave a margin.	Still more notes may be added as you write.
4. Analyse the question parts.	This leads to a line of argument.
5. State the line of argument.	This gives overall direction to the essay and helps the introduction.
6. Separate out main ideas or areas of knowledge and make them your subheadings.	Each may then take a paragraph in your final essay.
7. Fill in the facts, quotations, comments, thoughts which fit these subheadings.	These will form the main body of your essay.
8. Keep your notes near at hand.	You will need to search your notes for the details and materials you need.
9. Use reference and text books.	(a) To check your notes. (b) To search out extra information.

Table from p.88, *The History Manual* (Framework Press, 1985) by J. A. Cloake, V. Crinnion and S. M. Harrison

EXAMPLE

Look at the essay plan below:

ESSAY PLAN

"Food is a basic necessity of life, but over the last decade agricultural sectors have been declining in importance. It has therefore become necessary for governments to intervene." Discuss the ways in which the government can do this.

Introduction — (n.b. assessment — argument — transition)

1. Basic problem of agricultural sector
    — Unplanned fluctuations in output
        ⇒ price instability
           income instability

    — Cyclical fluctuations in prices (See Wood Ch. 4)

2. Agricultural stabilization programmes   (Wood Ch. 5)
    — Stabilization by govt. purchases
    — problems with stabilization policies
        — danger of creating excess supply
        — problems of price setting

3. Use of subsidies and price floors
    — explanation [use diagrams here]
    — problems of excess supply
        — EEC butter mountain / wine lake ⎫ See
        — sales to USSR etc.   ⎬ Economist
                                           ⎭ p. 67-9

4. Alternatives for the future   (Brown pp 76-81)
    — EEC — C.A.P
    — Increase in worldwide demand for foodstuffs
                = problems!

Conclusion , Bibliography

What are the good points about this plan?

(a) It is clearly structured into four main blocks. It begins by looking at the basic problem and progresses to looking at issues concerned with the future. It has a sensible and logical progression.

(b) Indentation has been used to separate the main points, and other points which are subsidiary.

(c) There is space for other points to be added as they occur to the writer.

(d) Notes are included showing where the use of diagrams might be appropriate.

(e) Some notes giving sources of information are included.

E. DRAFTING, RE-DRAFTING AND EDITING THE ESSAY

The techniques of drafting, re-drafting and editing are only really required in the first stages of your essay-writing. As you progress, your preparation and planning will improve until you can do away with this stage completely. Indeed, in the examination there is not time to go through this process. In the early stages, however, these techniques will give you confidence in your essay-writing.

Drafting and Re-drafting

Essays at A level and beyond impose new demands on your writing skills. You are required to do a lot of independent reading and in addition, essays need to be rather longer than was the case at GCSE. This raises problems in the early stages in the structuring of your essay.

It will be useful for you to approach your essay-writing in the first instance in two stages, making a first draft and a re-draft.

THE FIRST DRAFT

The first draft involves your writing largely for yourself, following your plan and making sure you have everything clear in your mind and subsequently clear on paper. At this stage you are clarifying your own ideas. You are not ready for other people's criticism.

Many people find that the hardest part of essay-writing is the first draft, where there are many problems to be overcome. The table on the next page pin-points some of these problems and makes suggestions for overcoming them.

PROBLEM	SOLUTION
1. Inability to get started.	(a) Try writing the first paragraph very quickly. This will help you get initial ideas flowing. Return to it and tidy it up later. (b) Try writing out one of your main arguments first, rather than the introduction.
2. Getting stuck part-way through.	(a) Look back at your plan. (b) Try having a short break. (c) Talk through the problem with somebody.
3. Finding part-way through that your note-making and reading has been inadequate.	(a) Go back and re-read. (b) Make sure you plan better in the future.
4. Losing the track of your argument.	(a) Have another look at your evidence and arguments. You may have misinterpreted them. (b) Go back to where you were confident of your argument and begin again from there. (c) Make sure you plan better in the future.
5. Running out of stamina.	(a) Have a break—are you working at the wrong time of the day? (b) Promise yourself a reward once you have finished.

RE-DRAFTING

Once your first draft is complete, put it down for a period of time, perhaps an hour or so, perhaps a couple of days. When you come back to the essay, you will be able to look at it more objectively.

When looking at your first draft again, you need to ask yourself:
(a) Does the essay fully answer the question?
(b) Are all the points relevant?
(c) Does the essay follow a logical progression?
(d) Does the essay read well—does it flow?
(e) Are all the arguments well-expressed and clear?
(f) Do the introduction and conclusion relate sensibly to the main body?

The following table should help you ask questions in order to identify *common problems* in the essay which may need attention:

Questions	Solutions and Strategies in Case of Problems
Scope and focus 1. Have you answered the question?	Look through your notes again. Confirm that your question analysis is appropriate. Read the draft, making notes in the margin where appropriate.
2. Have you covered all the important points in your reading?	List what you consider to be the main points and check that they are fully explained.
Logic and structure 3. Is there a clear argument running through the essay?	Construct a summary of the essay, based on paragraphs.
4. Does your essay have a sensible and effective introduction and conclusion?	Read the first and last paragraphs and check that there is a relationship between the two. Check that they also reflect the main concern of the essay title.

Many of these points are further expanded in section F. *Important Aspects of the essay.*

Editing

You are now almost ready to write out the final essay. You should not need to make any substantial revisions or extensions to your argument. But you should now look through your essay in the role of editor or proof-reader. Check for signs of inaccuracy, however small. The overall impression that you give by spending a little extra time at this stage can be far more professional. Carelessness can often detract from a serious consideration of the real arguments in your essay.

STRATEGIES FOR THE EDITING OF ESSAYS

1. Re-read the instructions and information contained in the essay title.
2. Read the essay carefully, and if possible ask someone else to read it as well, checking for silly mistakes.

3. Consult a dictionary or textbook if you are unsure about details.
4. Read passages of the essay aloud to see if they flow.
5. Check that your references are accurate.

F. IMPORTANT ASPECTS OF THE ESSAY

In this section we return to looking in more depth at some of the points which are very important in the *final presentation* of your essay. We are going to examine:

- The Introduction
- The Structure of the Essay
- Relevance
- Logical Argument
- Style and Presentation
- The Conclusion

You should fully master the material in this section before going on to write your essays.

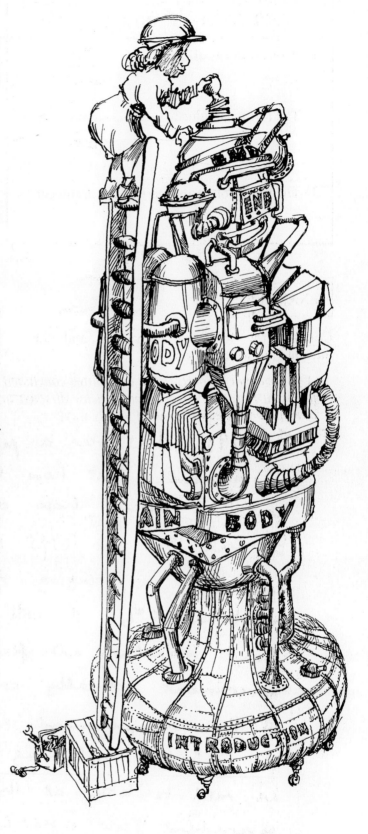

The Introduction

Every essay needs an introduction, a main body and conclusion. The middle, as we have seen, has to be the argument, discussion and consideration of the major points. These must directly answer the question set.

The introduction is an important and powerful part of the essay, not only because it sets the scene, but also because it gives the reader some idea of what to expect. Thus, if the introduction is well written and structured, you are giving a good impression to the reader, often the examiner!

The introduction should refer directly to the question, preparing the ground for the main body of the essay. It should also be a statement of intent and should lay out a path along which the essay should proceed. If you do not subsequently proceed along this path, that implies that you have not planned your essay with enough care.

—The introduction should be clear and interesting whilst not at the same time giving away your conclusions.

—It should ask questions which will subsequently be answered in the essay.

—We remember best what comes first and last when reading, thus the introduction and conclusion are the parts of your essays most likely to be remembered.

If you can satisfy the three requirements outlined on p.74, your introduction is at least structurally correct.

The style of that introduction is then up to you.

CONTENTS OF THE INTRODUCTION	FUNCTIONS
1. An assessment of the title	This should show that the writer has understood the topic under consideration and has a good grasp of the relevant material.
2. The line of argument	This should outline how the writer intends to proceed. This is the main function of the introduction but also shows that a question has been understood.
3. The transition to the start of the argument	This should allow a smooth movement to the first part of the main body and is the first stage in logical progression.

Adapted from p.92, *The History Manual* (Framework Press, 1985) by J. A. Cloake, V. Crinnion and S. M. Harrison

EXAMPLE

Consider the following essay title and the introduction which follows it:

A government all-party select committee concluded in 1985 that at least one million jobs had been lost as a result of government policies directed at inflation. To what extent do you agree that unemployment can be caused in this way?

The 1980s has been a period of very high unemployment. Just how high depends precisely how we define those counted as unemployed. Between 1980 and 1985 the government concentrated on bringing down the inflation rate to below 5%. It will be argued that the tight monetary and fiscal policy used by the government actually caused a large amount of the unemployment and indeed always will do. Before explaining that argument, however, we need to look at the reasons why the government saw inflation as its primary target.

Can you pin-point the assessment, the line of argument and the transitional sentence? In what ways might you have improved the introduction?

EXAMPLE

Consider the following essay title and the two different introductions which follow it.

'It is impossible to make accurate predictions about the price which will prevail in oligopoly markets, but it is clear that prices, once set, will tend to be relatively stable.' Discuss.

Introduction 1

An oligopoly is a situation where there are a few sellers in the market. They must be aware of each others actions. It will be shown in this essay that prices once set will be relatively stable. This will be done using the kinked demand curve theory.

Introduction 2

An oligopolistic market structure, where a few firms dominate a single market, is probably the commonest structure in the U.K. economy. There are many different theories of oligopoly and common to all of them is the recognition of mutual interdependence which a small number of firms creates. By looking at two of the most important theories we can assess the validity of the quotation. An examination of classic oligopoly markets will add some insight into the analysis.

General comments about the introductions:

Introduction 1

(a) The introduction is very short. It contains only four short sentences.

(b) The third sentence does not present a line of argument; it merely repeats part of the essay title.

(c) There is no indication that the writer really understands the topic under consideration. Indeed one gets the impression that all the writer might know about oligopoly is the kinked demand curve theory.

(d) There is no real transition into the main body of the essay.

(e) The introduction does not create a feeling of interest in the reader's mind. From the outset all that we seem to be getting is a potted account of one theory.

Introduction 2

(a) From the very start the writer gives the impression of knowing something about the topic by making the general comment 'probably the most common structure in the U.K. economy'. The fact that there are many theories of oligopoly is also recognised.

(b) The concept of mutual interdependence which is central to the essay is mentioned. Thus there is further evidence of understanding. This represents a very good assessment of the topic.

(c) A line of argument is clearly defined: two theories will be looked at, followed by an examination of the 'real world'. This also acts as a transition into the essay. The next paragraph would presumably begin looking at one of the theories.

(d) The introduction is a better length and, without being too involved, has a better style. From the outset it gives the impression that the writer has something interesting to discuss.

EXERCISE

(i) Look at the second introduction again. In what ways might you improve on it even further?

(ii) Using one of your recent essay titles, outline an introduction. Remember to use the three stages described above and try to develop some interest from the outset.

The Structure of the Essay

One of the most difficult things to achieve, when writing an essay, is a sound structure for the material you wish to present. A good essay plan, however, will put you well on the road to success.

Your general approach should be to hang some flesh on the general headings and sub-headings which you have made in your plan. Remember that if your plan follows a logical progression, so will your essay.

Each paragraph of your essay should deal with a specific theme or argument. When you have dealt with it, or are suggesting an alternative, go on to the next paragraph. Paragraphs should not be used decoratively. Some people find it useful to specify the number of paragraphs when they are planning; one paragraph for each major point, one for the introduction and one or two for the conclusion. This helps you to control the essay and to think concisely.

There is nothing worse than an essay which starts with one point, moves to the next and back to the first for no apparent reason. This gives the impression that the essay is being written as it comes into the writer's mind (which it probably is). You overcome this by having a plan and sticking to it.

Relevance

You should decide on the relevance of particular material at the same time as you go about selecting what to include in the essay. The inclusion or exclusion will depend on a number of aspects but if in doubt ask yourself the following questions:

—Is the material central to my argument?
—Does the material highlight the main points?
—Am I providing an example of a particular argument or situation by including the material?

or alternatively,

—Is the material there to fill up space?
—Does the material just repeat what I have already included?
—Is the material unconnected to the main body of my essay?

As you are writing your essay, you should keep referring back to the essay title, your question analysis and your plan. This will ensure that you do not let your argument go off at an irrelevant tangent.

The decision as to what to include or not include will get easier to make with experience. Ultimately, the decision will be based on your understanding of Economics. This means that it is important that you read, discuss and think. The more you practise essay writing, the better you will become at selecting relevant material.

Logical Argument

As well as selecting relevant material, you must present it in a logical and clear way. The most important thing to remember is that every idea, observation or argument must be supported by facts or reasons. As has been said, each paragraph should deal with a separate argument and these should be arranged in a logical progression so that your essay moves smoothly from one point to another.

Don't worry if pieces of information or arguments conflict. Indeed, where this is the case, you have the opportunity to write a particularly interesting essay. You will rarely find a single strand of argument in Economics anyway, because there are so many opposing views. The important thing to remember is that, whatever your conclusion, it must be justified. If your conclusion is that the opposing arguments are all strong, then say so. Economists themselves are very fond of using the words '...thus more research needs to be done in this area before we can come to a definitive conclusion.'

If, on the other hand, you consider that one set of arguments is much stronger than another, you should be able to argue this from an unbiased point of view. If a strong set of arguments leads you to a particular conclusion, that is fine so long as the alternatives have been considered in a fair and consistent way. An essay based on prejudice and misinformation is not a good piece of work. Usually the evidence or argument against your point of view will be dealt with first.

The essay may well progress according to one of the following simple formats:

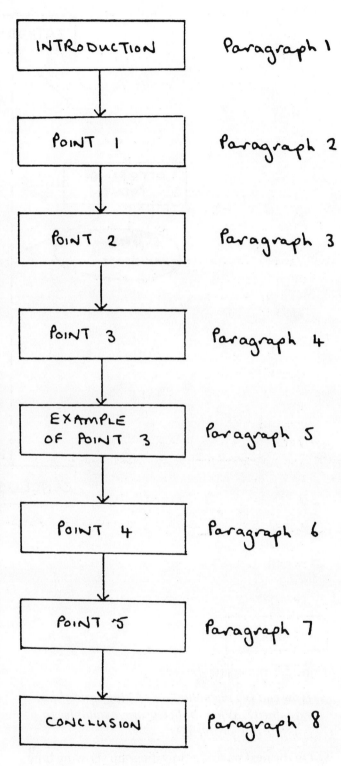

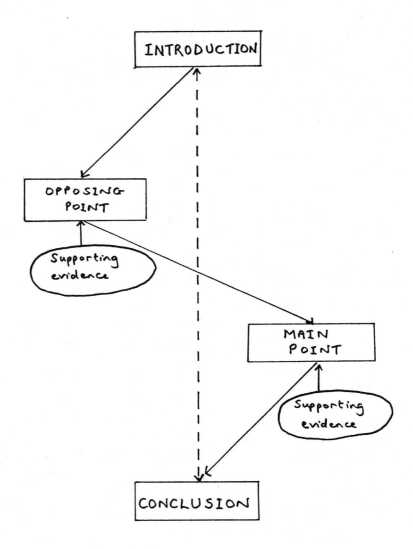

EXAMPLE

Consider the essay:

How can the phenomenon of 'stagflation' be explained? What policies are available to combat this problem?

On the next page is a flow diagram showing how the main argument can be linked together in a logical way.

How can the phenomenon of 'stagflation' be explained? What policies are available to combat this problem?

① ┌─────────────────────────────┐
   │ Introduction   │
   └─────────────────────────────┘

② ┌─────────────────────────────┐   Order in
   │ Definition of stagflation: │   essay is
   │ High Inflation   │   numbered
   │ High Unemployment   │
   │ Poor growth   │
   └─────────────────────────────┘

EXPLANATIONS		
Keynesian	Monetarist	Marxist
③ Major disequilibrium But cannot really explain.	④ 1. Phillips curve slopes forward 2. Cause is misuse of fiscal policy 3. And loose monetary policy	⑤ Analysis of the business cycle shows stagflation to be the result of capitalism
POLICIES		
⑥ Simple Keynesian model does not appear to have a solution	⑦ Concentrate on inflation Use tight monetary policy Concentrate on supply-side	⑧ Abandon capitalism

⑨ ┌─────────────────────────────┐
   │ Conclusions   │
   │ – must be monetarist   │
   │   or Marxist!?   │
   └─────────────────────────────┘

How does this sort of structure help logical development?

1. The essay begins with an introduction and definition of terms, broadens out into a discussion of explanations and policies and ends with a conclusion.
2. Three attempts at an explanation are developed, compared and contrasted with each other.
3. Possible policies which follow on from the explanations are then discussed; thus theory is discussed first, followed by application of that theory.
4. The numbers follow a logical order, each one accounting for one or two paragraphs.
5. The conclusion stems from the discussion, abandoning one line of thought but leaving open the decision as to which of the other two offers the better explanation and set of policies.
6. The whole approach is very structured and leaves little opportunity for the writer to stray away from the point.

EXERCISE

Go through a couple of the essay titles in this chapter and sketch out similar diagrams, paying particular attention to the logical flow of information.

Style and Presentation

Everyone's style of writing is different. Reading would become very boring if our styles were all the same. Nevertheless, when writing Economics essays, there are some general points to remember. Style is important because it reflects the way you project yourself to the reader. We have already noted that a poor style may lead the reader to believe that you are weak on understanding.

A common rule to be adopted is the ABC of style:

    Accuracy
    Brevity
    Clarity

Brevity and clarity can be achieved by making sure that you follow a logical progression and that you do not include irrelevant information. There are two aspects of accuracy which you should concentrate on. Firstly, your Economics should be factually accurate. Do not include material which you are not sure about in an essay, but go away and read around subjects until you have thoroughly checked the facts and evidence you are presenting.

The second type of accuracy to pay attention to is accuracy of grammar and spelling. No one expects that you will never make a mistake of this kind, but too many errors create a bad impression.

PUNCTUATION

A common problem for students who begin writing advanced technical essays is deciding where sentences should begin and end and where paragraphs should begin and end.

As a general rule:

(i) Each paragraph should contain a separate argument
(ii) Sentences should not be overlong
(iii) You should avoid complex sub-clauses
(iv) If information can be written more clearly using two sentences rather than one, then that should be done. On the other hand, avoid a lot of very short, sharp sentences as these tend to give the impression of immaturity in your writing.

EXERCISE

Here are two essay passages which are almost identical. Read them both and comment on their style in the light of points (i) to (iv) on p.80.

Paragraph A

Oligopoly may be defined as an industry in which there are a few firms and many buyers. However, this definition begs two important questions: First, how many is few? Broadly speaking, the number of firms should be sufficiently small for there to be 'conscious interdependence'. In other words, each firm should be aware that its future prospects depend not only on its own policies, but also on those of its rivals. Second, what is an industry? In theory, an industry is defined as a group of firms whose products are close substitutes for each other. That is to say, the products have high and positive cross-elasticities of demand. In practice, precise calculations of cross-elasticities of demand are impossible to make. An industry is then defined either by approximate similarity of output or by similarity of a major input.

Paragraph B

Oligopoly may be defined as an industry in which there are a few firms and many buyers, but, this definition begs two important questions: First, how many is few? Broadly speaking, the number of firms should be sufficiently small for there to be 'conscious interdependence', with each firm aware that its future prospects depend not only on its own policies but also on the policies of its rivals. Second, what is an industry? In theory, an industry is defined as a group of firms whose products are close substitutes for one another, that is, where the products have high and positive cross-elasticities of demand, although in practice precise calculations of cross-elasticities of demand are impossible to make, and an industry is defined either by approximate similarity of output or by similarity of the major input.

SPELLING

Incorrect spelling will not lose you marks. But bad spelling does create a bad impression, especially when words central to Economics are misspelt. Check in a dictionary if you are unsure about particular spellings and try to remember the correct spellings—we are all continually learning. Reading widely will also help your spelling, particularly of the more technical words often used in Economics.

Here is a list of the more common words used in Economics which are often misspelt:

accelerator	industrialisation
aggregate	inflationary
autonomous	opportunity
bureaucracy	permanent
business	protectionism
commodity	quantitative
deficit	sufficient
efficiency	technological
indifference	transmission

ABBREVIATIONS

It is good practice to use abbreviations when taking notes, but abbreviations should not be used when you are writing essays. An essay is a formal piece of writing in which words should be written in full.

APPEARANCE

Your final essay should, at the very least, be clear, tidy and legible. You should not spend time on the final presentation of the essay to the detriment of the content, but there are simple points you can remember:

● Leave a wide margin for tutor's comments
● Leave space for comments at the end of the essay
● Keep a copy of your essay, in case the original is lost
● Check to see if you are required to use a specific layout for the essay

Some people have difficulty with handwriting, especially in examination conditions, but handwriting like that in the example on p.83 is useless.

An examiner will not spend time trying to decipher it, so you will have wasted your time.

If your writing is hard to read, try the following activity:

(a) Give a specimen of your handwriting to a couple of friends. Ask them to underline any letters or combinations of letters which they find difficult to read.
(b) Get your friends to tell you what it is about these underlined parts which causes difficulty, e.g. words crowded or loops from one line getting tangled with the next.
(c) Analyse your problems in (a) and (b) and practise putting them right. When you think you have solved the problems, return to (a).

REFERENCES AND BIBLIOGRAPHY

You should carefully acknowledge any ideas you have borrowed from other sources and list these at the end of your essay, in the bibliography. Never copy sentences from books unless you put them in quotes and acknowledge their source.

References should be listed in alphabetical order and the information outlined in section D (p.63) should be included.

The Conclusion

The purpose of the conclusion is to remind the reader of what you have accomplished in the main body of the essay. It should contain two elements:

● A brief restatement of your main argument
● An indication of how this conclusion differs from or qualifies the essay title, with perhaps some reference back to the introduction

The conclusion should satisfy the reader that you have answered the question. You should avoid just tacking something on to the end as if the essay should be 'gift-wrapped'. Your conclusion must convey a clear indication of what preceded it.

Remember that it should be possible for a reader to look only at the introduction and the conclusion in order to get some idea of what is contained in your answer.

It really is pointless writing an essay which cannot be read — it really is pointless wasting your time. No one can read it so why bother?

If you do write badly then do something about it! Give a specimen of your writing to a friend and ask them to underline words or letters which they cannot read. Analyse your problems and put them right.

Can you read what is written here? Its worse than most, but it does prove a point.

G. ASSESSMENT AND FOLLOW-UP

Handing in a completed essay should not be seen as the end of the process. Remember that the essay is a learning exercise and that even more can be learned after the essay has been marked and handed back.

There are three points at which you can start analysing how effectively you handled the piece of writing and begin to weigh up what improvements could have been made:

—the assessment of your work by the marker;
—your self-assessment;
—discussion with other students.

Remember that there is no such thing as a perfect essay.

Assessment by the Marker

1. The grade or mark
Your first response on receiving a piece of marked work is to look first for the grade it was given. This represents a judgement on your performance and is an evaluation of the quality of your work. It is not a judgement on your capacities, merely how you did on the particular essay in question.

2. Written comments
The written comments on your essay should be of more use to you than the mark. Comments in the margin will usually deal with specific points, such as inaccuracies. At the end there will be more general points, commenting on the emphasis you have put on your answer, and your style. Often there will be strategies for improving your essay next time.

EXAMPLE

Below is an extract from an essay where students have been asked to discuss the effects of multinational companies on world trade. Note the type of comments which have been made by the marker. Would you have added any others?

You should be able to see that the comments are aimed at helping the student. The comments pinpoint areas which can be improved. You should therefore take time to analyse comments and should respond to them either by doing extra reading where you have left gaps or thinking about how you might have approached the essay from a different angle. Comments should be seen as part of your continual process of learning.

International competitiveness depends on firms being able to export anywhere in the world. Traditionally the U.K. has exported capital-intensive goods and other countries specialising in goods according to their comparative advantage.

have specialised

do countries really do this in practice??

In the past it has tended to be the case that just as in perfect competition, no single firm can have an impact on the market, so it was that because the world was so big, no firm could influence world trade. But some economists now believe that the multinational sector of the economy has grown so fast that this is no longer the case. Large multinational, sometimes called transnational firms can operate across a number of countries.

Can you name any?

or group (e.g. EEC)

Investment in any single country is often not undertaken without significant government encouragement even when the firm is making enough profits to invest anyway. A good example of this sort of encouragement was seen in the U.K. with the establishment of the Nissan car factory in the North East. — *More details? What sort of help?*

But is this not done for the good of the country?

Others argue that because multinational companies have subsidiaries in many countries they can to some extent control the imports and exports of that a country, requiring subsidiaries to buy from one particular source and not another. In this way free trade does not come about. The multinational companies can be said to create a certain degree of interdependence and force the world economy to a more oligopolistic situation rather than a competitive one.

That is a good point

3. *Personal discussion*

In some cases you may require more explanation as to why certain parts of your essay were not seen as totally appropriate. Although a personal discussion with your teacher may seem a little daunting at first, it often represents the most useful feedback you can get. It gives you a chance to explain your ideas more thoroughly, explain any problems you have, and discuss possible improvements to the presentation of the essay.

Self-Assessment

In order to assess your own work and to improve your strategies for the future it is helpful to ask yourself the following questions:

(a) How efficient were my reading strategies? Did I spend too long on general reading materials? Did I miss an important source?

(b) How useful were my notes? Did they cover too much material? Did they leave out essential details?

(c) Was the time I spent on thinking and planning well spent? How representative was my final essay of the original plan?

(d) Did I start the writing stage too soon or too late?

(e) Should I have allowed more time for re-drafting and editing?

Discussion with other Students

A frequently neglected strategy is to discuss your work with your fellow students. Often it is a good idea to form an essay-swapping group. In this way you can see which essay-writing strategies were successful and which were not.

The Essay-Writing Process

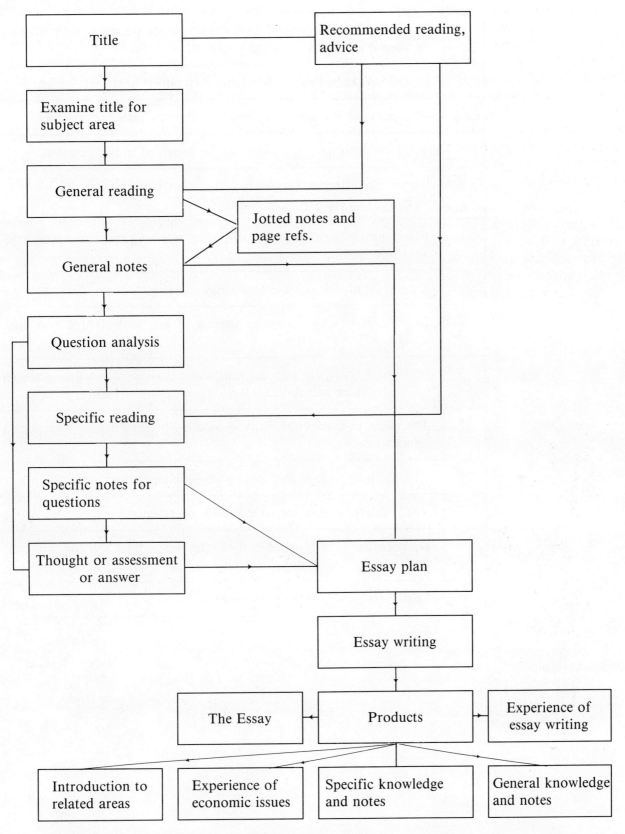

(This flow chart shows the student's unaided progress in producing an essay from being given a title and reading list.)

Adapted from p.108, *The History Manual* (Framework Press, 1985) by J. A. Cloake, V. Crinnion and S. M. Harrison

H. CHECKLIST   √ √ √ √ √ √ √ √ √ √ √

1	Your ability to use your knowledge and understanding of Economics to answer a specific question is crucial.
2	Questions can be broken down into their constituent parts for analysis.
3	Paraphrasing the question can bring the key factor to the fore.
4	Look for information which may be provided in the question.
5	There are different approaches to essay-writing. These are likely to alter as your essay-writing improves.
6	Plan your essay carefully by collecting, selecting and structuring relevant information.
7	Do not be afraid to leave something out if it does not fit.
8	In your early stages of essay-writing, draft, re-draft and edit your essay.
9	Make sure that your introduction, main body and conclusion are all linked together and reflect a well-argued essay structure.
10	The main part of your essay should be presented in a logical and interesting way.
11	Check your spellings just as you would check your facts.
12	Read widely to improve your style and presentation.
13	Do not treat your finished essay as the end of your learning exercise. Follow up points made when the essay has been marked.
14	Learn from every essay you write.

HANDLING DATA

CHAPTER

4

Page

A.   WHAT DO WE MEAN BY 'HANDLING DATA'? 90

B.   CAN YOU BE MISLED BY STATISTICS? 91

C.   SOURCES OF DATA 93
  Statistical Sources 93
  Other Sources 94

D.   INTERPRETING DATA 94
  Statistics 94
    1. Trends 94
    2. Relationships 96
  Graphs and Charts 98
  Textual Information 100

E.   HANDLING THE DATA-RESPONSE QUESTION 103
  What is Expected of You? 103
  Tackling the Question 103
  Writing the Answer 103

F.   CHECKLIST 114

G.   END OF CHAPTER EXERCISES 115

A. WHAT DO WE MEAN BY 'HANDLING DATA'

Economists cannot perform controlled experiments in laboratories as scientists can. The only way for the economist to verify theories is to examine the real world. Thus, we need to collect data from the real world and examine it, in order to find out if theories are supported by evidence.

When data is referred to here, it means any information of a quantitative or non-quantitative nature, including extracts from articles, newspaper reports, economic statistics and balance sheets.

There are a large number of ways in which we can examine data and you are required to be able to carry out many of these. Often data will not be exactly in the form we want and therefore it will be necessary to adjust it.

Much of the data used by economists is in the form of economic statistics. You will be required to examine and interpret these statistics throughout your course. There is a popular belief that statistics can be made to prove anything. This is quite untrue, although there are techniques often used, and examined below, which may make statistics *appear* to prove anything. It is important, therefore, that statistics are handled and interpreted very carefully, so that you do not jump to the wrong conclusions.

B. CAN YOU BE MISLED BY STATISTICS?

Before progressing further let us see if you yourself can be misled by the presentation of data.

EXERCISE

Below are a number of questions for you to answer. When you have worked through them, see if you were correct by looking at the *Answers* section.

(a) Figure 1 shows sales figures for a firm with four products. Is it correct that sales of product B are twice the sales of product C?

Figure 1

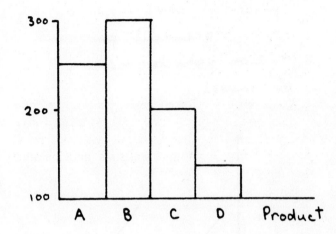

(b) Figure 2 gives sales data for two firms. Which firm has the fastest rate of growth of sales?

Figure 2

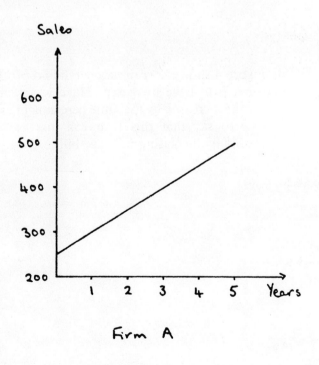

Firm A

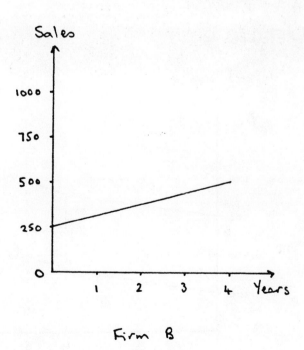

Firm B

Figure 3

Number of cars involved in an accident per million vehicle miles of travel

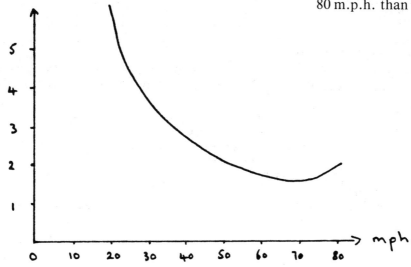

(c) Given the information provided in figure 3, is it correct to say that it is safer to travel at 80 m.p.h. than at 35 m.p.h.?

Figure 4

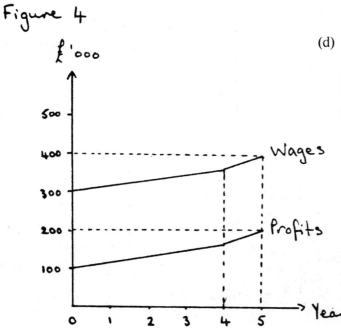

(d) Figure 4 shows how the wage bill and profits for a firm have increased. Have wages and profits increased by the same percentage? Is it true to say that this firm will increase its profits by increasing its wage bill?

ANSWERS

(a) Do not be misled by the scale. Although the height of the bar representing product B is twice that of product C, it does not mean that there have been twice as many sales of product B. Note that sales for B and C are 300 and 200 respectively.

(b) Again, do not be misled by the scales. Firm A and Firm B have identical increases in sales. But Firm B has achieved this in four years, while Firm A has taken five years. Thus firm B has the faster growth rate.

(c) It is certainly not the case that it is safer to travel at 80 m.p.h. Fewer accidents occur when people travel at 80 m.p.h. because fewer people travel at that speed. Most people travel at an average speed of 30–35 m.p.h. and we can therefore expect more accidents at that speed. The ideal measure would be to find out what percentage of people driving at each particular speed have accidents. Can you predict the shape of the graph?

(d) Although the lines are parallel, the percentage increases in wages and profits are not the same. The wage bill has increased from 300 to 400 (i.e. by 33.3%) and profits have increased from 100 to 200 (i.e. by 100%). We cannot possibly argue that higher wages can lead to higher profits on the basis of the diagram. We need information about all other factors which influence wages and profits.

You will realise now that the presentation of data can be very misleading. Advertisers often use the methods tried above to give favourable impressions for their clients. Often scales on graphs are completely missing, which makes the information impossible to decipher. It is therefore vital that you look at all information you are given in a critical way. Examine everything carefully so as not to fall into the many traps left for you.

C. SOURCES OF DATA

This section is intended to highlight some of the more useful and easily accessible sources of statistics and other information about the U.K., European and World economies. They can all be obtained through your local library. Larger libraries will keep them in their statistics collection.

Statistical Sources

1. *Guide to Official Statistics* (Her Majesty's Stationery Office)
If you are looking for statistics about a particular topic, this is the first place to look. This guide lists all the government statistics, presented by subject area, for example, housing, employment, capital accumulation, income and expenditure.

2. *Annual Abstract of Statistics* (Central Statistical Office)
This contains 400 tables of annual statistics for the previous ten years. It presents the major statistics from each of the government departments.

3. *Business Monitor* (Business Statistics Office)
Information is provided about a number of different industries, usually for a four-year period. This is particularly useful if you are doing a project about a particular industry or sector of the economy.

4. *Economic Trends* (CSO)
This statistical source is published monthly and contains tables and charts illustrating trends in the U.K. economy. Data is provided monthly, quarterly and on an annual basis.

5. *Employment Gazette* (Department of Employment)
This is a monthly publication by the Department of Employment. Each edition contains data on employment, unemployment, industrial disputes, earnings and retail prices. Special features are also included, looking at specific issues relating to the labour market.

6. *Regional Trends* (CSO)
Regional Trends contains economic, social and population statistics relating to regions within the U.K. economy.

7. *U.K. Balance of Payments* (CSO)
Often called 'the pink book', this source contains statistics on all aspects of the balance of payments. Data for a ten-year period is provided for purposes of comparison.

8. *Economic Survey of Europe* (HMSO)
Data is presented on each of the European Countries, the EEC and the Eastern bloc. Information is displayed very clearly in tables and charts with clearly written discussion.

9. *I.M.F. World Economic Outlook* (HMSO)
This annual publication presents projections for individual countries around the world, as well as looking at key policy issues in the world economy.

10. *U.N. Statistical Yearbook* (HMSO)
This looks particularly at a variety of statistics in terms of developed and developing countries.

Addresses:
HMSO (Her Majesty's Stationery Office)
P.O. Box 569
London SE1 9NH

CSO (Central Statistical Office)
P.O. Box 569
London SE1 9NH

Business Statistics Office
Cardiff Office
Newport
Gwent NPT 1XG

Department of Employment
Caxton House
Tothill Street
London SW1H 9NF

Other Sources

1. *Bank reviews*
Each of the major banks produces a quarterly review. These contain articles about a range of applied economic issues. They are available free of charge, on application.
   Write to the following addresses:
      Barclays Review. Group Economics Department, 54 Lombard Street, London. EC3P 3AH
      Lloyds Bank Review. Lloyds Bank plc, 71 Lombard Street, London. EC3P 3BS
      Midland Bank Review. Public Relations Department, Midland Bank, P.O. Box 2, Griffin House, Silver Street Head, Sheffield. S1 3GG
      National Westminster Bank Quarterly Review. 41 Lothbury, London. EC2P 2BP
      The Three Banks Review. The Royal Bank of Scotland, Edinburgh. EH2 0DG

2. *Economic Progress Report*
Published monthly by the Treasury, providing current statistics and comment about the U.K. economy. Available from The Central Office of Information, Hercules Road, London. SE1 7DU.

3. *Lloyds Bank Economic Bulletin*
This is another free monthly publication. Each issue looks at a topical area of applied Economics. This is particularly valuable for students at the start of their studies since it is written for non-economists. Write to Lloyds Bank at the address above.

D.   INTERPRETING DATA

The way you approach your data analysis will partly depend on the type of data which you are expected to make use of, but as a general rule, bear the following points in mind at all times:
(a) Think about the application of economic theory and concepts to the data you are given.
(b) Think carefully about what the data tells you and remember that it will need to be transferred into your words.
(c) Use the data that is of most benefit to you. There will often be material included which is not directly relevant.

Statistics

People often find statistical data difficult to handle. Nothing very difficult is involved in looking at data and A level students are not expected to do difficult statistical manipulations. Basically, you should look for two things when examining a set of statistics:
   1. TRENDS
   2. RELATIONSHIPS

1. TRENDS

You can consider a trend to be an approximate path which statistics may follow. Ask yourself if the statistics you are examining are rising or falling, or rising then falling, or whether there is a trend at all. Economists are very interested in examining trends in order to be able to predict the path of an economy or a firm in the future.
   It is often the case that trends are difficult to spot. If you are looking at time-series data (statistics over a period of time) then it can be useful to do a simple plot of the data to see trends more clearly. Be careful not to spend time doing this if it is not necessary in an examination, however.

EXAMPLE

Below are three sets of growth figures for three different economies. Look at them carefully and
think about any trends which are apparent. Then
look at the first graph plot which shows the growth
path of the three economies.

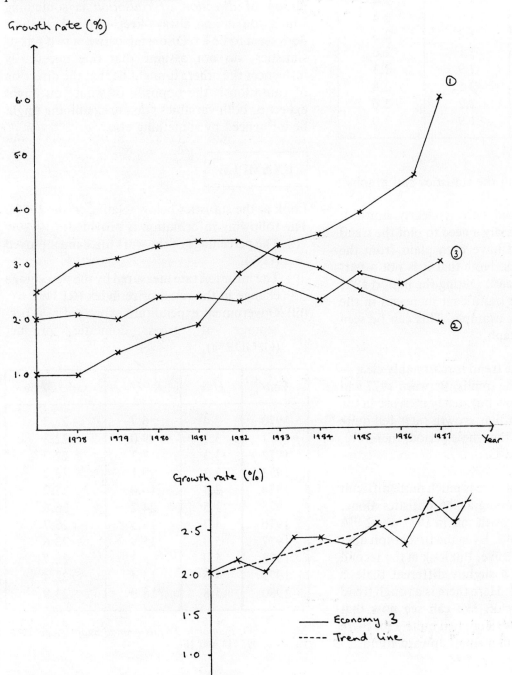

Growth rates (%)

Year	Economy 1	Economy 2	Economy 3
1977	1.0	2.5	2.0
1978	1.0	3.0	2.1
1979	1.4	3.1	2.0
1980	1.7	3.3	2.4
1981	1.9	3.4	2.4
1982	2.8	3.4	2.3
1983	3.3	3.1	2.6
1984	3.5	2.9	2.3
1985	3.9	2.5	2.8
1986	4.6	2.2	2.6
1987	6.0	1.9	3.0

Things to note from the statistics and graphs:

Economy 1: The trend here is clearly upward; indeed there was hardly a need to plot the trend at all, as it should have been plain from the statistics themselves. Note that it is not a particularly smooth trend. During the period 1981 to 1983 there were significant increases in the rate of growth, for example. This can be seen clearly from the graph.

Economy 2: Again the trend is reasonably clear—or more precisely the trends. Between 1977 and 1982 there was a slow but steady increase in the growth rates. After that growth rates fell quite dramatically. Over the whole period, therefore, growth rates fell.

Economy 3: The trend here is much more difficult to determine by looking at the statistics alone. But note that the growth rate in 1977 was 2.0% and in 1987 was 3.0%. Even the first graph does not look very conclusive. But look at the second graph plot, where a slightly different scale is used for economy 3. Here there is a rough trend line fitted to the plot. We can see now that although the figures fluctuated quite a lot there was nevertheless still a small upward trend.

2. RELATIONSHIPS

If you are asked to consider more than one set of statistics, look to see if there is any simple relationship between the two. For example, does one set of statistics fall every time another one rises, or do the statistics rise and fall together?

When looking at simple relationships, the notion of *direction of causation* is something which you should always keep in mind. If there does seem to be a relationship between two sets of statistics, do not assume that one necessarily influences the other. It might be that the direction of causation is the opposite of what you might expect or both variables you are examining might be influenced by something else.

EXAMPLE

Look at the statistics below relating to the 1970s. The following information is provided:
  (i) The percentage of the workforce unemployed (U%).
 (ii) The inflation rate measured by the percentage change in the retail price index (RPI%).
(iii) Government expenditure expressed as a percentage of gross domestic product (G/GDP%).

Year	U%	RPI%	G/GDP%
1970	2.4	6.7	22.3
1971	3.1	9.0	22.3
1972	3.3	7.3	22.7
1973	2.3	9.1	23.2
1974	2.3	16.0	25.2
1975	3.5	24.2	26.6
1976	4.7	16.5	25.7
1977	5.0	15.9	23.6
1978	5.0	8.3	22.7
1979	4.6	13.4	22.4
1980	5.8	18.0	23.9

Source: CSO, *Economic Trends Annual Supplement,* 1984, Tables 8, 99, 114 and 162.

1. Trends

Notice that unemployment has been rising steadily throughout the period, except for slight falls in 1973 and 1979. Thus the trend is clearly upwards.

The inflation rate rose quite rapidly from 1970 to 1975, fell back from 1975 to 1978 and then rose again. If there are any trends to be observed, then there is a rise up to 1975, a fall to 1978 and a further rise thereafter. In other words there seems to be a sort of wave pattern. However, serious words of warning must be considered here. A trend is hardly a trend if it only covers a small number of observations or a short period. We really need more information here. Monthly or quarterly data might help us detect trends more clearly.

G/GDP% fluctuated between 22.3 and 26.6 but was at a peak in 1975. There does not seem to be a clear trend at all here.

2. Relationships

There seems to be no obvious relationship between unemployment and inflation. We might have expected this if we had been thinking about the existence of a Phillips curve relationship.

Notice that the highest level of inflation occurs when we have the highest level of G/GDP%. Moreover it seems to be the case that these two variables rise and fall with each other. We cannot be sure about the direction of causation though. It would be dangerous therefore to try to reach any conclusions about this.

EXERCISE

Try to answer the following questions based on the statistics above, before having a look at the outline answers which are provided.

(a) What can we say about the effectiveness of government expenditure in reducing unemployment? Does this government expenditure have any effect on the economy?

(b) What factors not covered by the statistics could account for the high inflation rate in 1975?

(c) Try to find some current statistics for these variables. To what extent are they different for the 1980s?

ANSWERS

(a) The conclusion seems to be that an expansionary fiscal stance, implying an increase in G/GDP%, does not have the impact on unemployment which a Keynesian approach to the economy might predict. The expansion seems to find its way quite rapidly into the inflation rate. Remember, though, that to make a more detailed judgement we really need to look at other data.

(b) Basically there are two other factors which we need to take into account:
   (i) the quadrupling in oil prices in 1973/4:
   (ii) significant increases in the money supply in 1982/3.

EXERCISE

(a) From the statistics presented on p.98, assess the validity of the commonly cited 'North-South divide'.

(b) What differences in the characteristics of the unemployed are there between the North and the South?

Source: *Lloyds Bank
Economic Bulletin,*
May 1987.

Table 1
Regional performance. Ranked by gdp per head.

	Gdp per head 1985	Personal disposable income per head, 1985	Real personal disposable income growth per head, 1975-85	Unemployment % of working population Jan 1987	Long term unemployed % of unemployed Jan 1987
South East	5831	4725	19.92	8.5	36.2
East Anglia	5118	4244	26.21	9.3	33.5
Scotland	4942	4181	20.86	15.1	39.2
North West	4877	4074	16.95	14.3	44.3
E. Midlands	4861	4066	18.46	11.4	39.2
South West	4763	4152	21.34	10.4	32.7
North	4717	3919	18.24	16.9	44.3
W. Midlands	4690	3997	10.24	13.8	46.3
Yorks & Humb	4662	3923	17.70	13.8	42.0
Wales	4509	3778	14.27	14.3	40.6
N. Ireland	3799	3538	18.67	19.3	50.0

Source: Economic Trends, Employment Gazette.

Graphs and Charts

Graphs and charts are often used to present material in a clear and concise way. Indeed, you will almost certainly make use of them yourself in your work. So long as you make sure that you clearly understand what is being presented, these can often be more easily interpreted than lists of statistics. The problem comes when insufficient data is provided or when the statistics are being presented in such a way as to try to mislead you. With more practice, you should be able to spot this. Think back to the exercises you did in section B.

Points to remember:

- If scales are being used, make sure that you cannot be misled by them.
- Read footnotes to charts carefully. Often simplifying assumptions will have been made which you need to be aware of.
- If shading has been used, make sure you understand why.
- Do not let visual impressions obscure the facts. Look at the graph or chart carefully and critically.
- If there is a break in the series of statistics, it should be pointed out. This means that the statistics before and after the break are not strictly comparable.

EXAMPLE

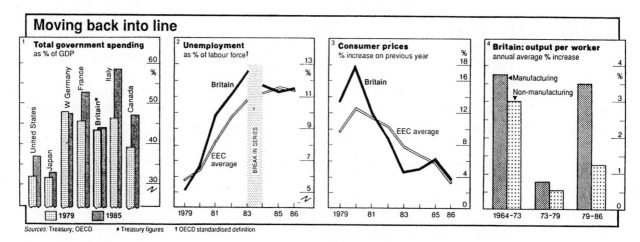

The Economist, 23 May, 1987

Let us make an assessment of the performance of the U.K. economy between 1979 and 1986:

1. *Total government spending:*
   Government spending is given as a percentage of GDP. Note that different shadings are used for 1979 and 1985. Britain seems to find itself in the middle of a ranking of spending nations. Ask yourself if the statistics were chosen deliberately to show this, however. What we can see is that all the nations except West Germany increased their spending as a percentage of GDP between 1979 and 1985 and that Britain's increase seems to be the smallest of the increases. Whether you consider this to be good or bad depends on your perspective.

2. *Unemployment:*
   Unemployment as a percentage of the labour force is shown for Britain and for the EEC average. Notice in particular the break in the series in 1983 caused by the government's reassessment of the methods used to count the unemployed. Figures before and after the break are not strictly comparable, therefore. Before the break, the percentage unemployed in Britain was significantly higher than the EEC average. We probably need more data to be able to comment about differences after the break.

3. *Consumer prices:*
   The percentage increase in consumer prices in Britain is measured against the EEC average. This time it is easier to make comparisons. Before 1981, Britain had higher increases in consumer prices than the EEC average, between 1981 and 1985, they were lower, and after that just slightly higher. It would have been useful to know whether the measure of the percentage increase in consumer prices in Britain was the retail price index or some other index.

4. *Output per worker:*
   Statistics are only presented for Britain, and different shading is used for the manufacturing sector and the non-manufacturing sector. The annual average increase in output per worker is given for three time periods. Be careful not to interpret the figures as absolute levels. They do not indicate that output per worker was lower in 1973–1979 than in 1964–1973. Indeed, because the percentage increases are all positive, this indicates a steady increase in output per worker throughout the whole period. What we can say is that the increase in output per worker was fastest in the earliest time period.

EXERCISE

Look through a recent copy of *The Economist* or a quality newspaper (e.g. *The Guardian, The Independent, The Daily Telegraph, The Times*). Find some information presented as a graph or chart and ask yourself the following questions:

(a) Is the information presented in a convenient, understandable and clear form?

(b) Is the explanation of the graph or chart helpful? Does the explanation claim anything which is not really shown?

(c) What is the graph or chart telling you? Is this a sensible way to put over the information?

(d) How might the presentation or content of the information be improved?

A SIMPLE GRAPH

Textual Information

The key to using text in data analysis is to comprehend fully what you are reading about. It is worthwhile spending time carefully reading information provided, so as not to miss important points. Often you may be given passages or articles to consider in which the information you need is only one part of the whole. But at other times relevant information will be spread throughout the text.

In a data-response question you will often be asked one or two questions about the text itself and then a supplementary question which will require you to add your own knowledge to the answer.

A possible strategy for reading textual information:

(a) Glance at the material in a cursory way. Read the first paragraph and the last paragraph.
(b) Briefly look at the questions which follow the text to get an idea of the subject matter which is being examined.
(c) Read through the whole passage, bearing the questions in mind.
(d) Look at the questions in detail, considering how you might approach them.
(e) Read the passage through once more, making notes in the margins and underlining important points or sentences which it might be useful to quote.

Note that a general strategy for approaching all types of data response question is given in section E. You will have to develop a precise strategy yourself, which should come with practice.

EXAMPLE

Follow the strategy above in reading the article
below and answering the questions which follow.

The sell to the swell

After yuppies, what next? If advertisers listened to their market researchers, they ought to be targeting the growing number of swells: smart-women-earning-lots-in-London.

In 1985, 16% of the Nationwide building society's mortgage lending went to women—a figure that has doubled in the past ten years. In London, the proportion was 24%, and in some London boroughs, such as Kensington and Chelsea, Islington, and Camden, women were well over a third of all borrowers. Other figures from the Nationwide show that most of the increase has come from women new to the housing market. Half of all women borrowers were first-time buyers, compared with 40% of men. And 56% were single, compared with only a quarter of men.

Most of these financially independent women have not started families. But even women who already have children control enormous spending power. The Henley Centre for Forecasting estimates that working women aged 25 to 44 with families have £11.3 billion of income at their disposal, their earnings topped up by child benefit. This should rise over the next few years as mothers have fewer children and go back to work more quickly after having their babies.

A study by the creative research unit at J. Walter Thompson (JWT) divides women of working age into housewives (52%) and working women (48%). It then splits the housewives into "stay-at-home" and "plan-to-work" groups—38% and 15% respectively—and the working women into "just-a-job" (30%) and "career-minded" (18%).

Unsurprisingly, the career-minded women travel and eat out more, are more likely to have cars, credit cards and microwave ovens, and spend more on their appearance. But even the housewives are a far cry from those of 20 or 30 years ago. Most had a job before they married and plan to go back to work once their children are older. They see looking after a home as a job and resent the fact that society seems to devalue it.

Has advertising kept up with these changes? Yes and no. Gone are the unashamedly sexist TV ads of the 1950s and 1960s where women slaved over their cooking all day for the reward of a word of praise from hubby when he returned from work. But TV commercials can still be far more old-fashioned in their assumptions than the soap operas between which they are sandwiched.

This annoys and frustrates women in all the JWT groups. They dislike female stereotypes, whether it is the perfect housewife and mother or the sassy working woman. Dressing a fashion model in a suit and giving her a briefcase works only if she looks intelligent enough for the part. Conversely, some "housewife" ads can be successful if they are well-characterised. A recent ad for Oxo comes in for a lot of praise because the mother is intelligent and witty, has the measure of her family and is eminently believable.

Most criticised (though, to be fair, a tiny minority of ads) are commercials for washing powders, washing-up liquids and soaps. Women object to the assumption that they are only, or particularly, interested in getting clothes or dishes cleaner or whiter. And they dislike ads which make women seem stupid or unable to make proper decisions. Two examples from the research:

"It irritates me. The idea that women would talk about washing powder. You might comment on the softness but not that much. It goes over the top. It suggests that women have a lower intelligence." (Plan-to-work housewife).

"It makes me wonder if these ads are made by men. It's what they *think* women say to each other." (Stay-at-home housewife)

She's right. Almost all the ads are made by men. Ms Lynda MacDonnell of Aspect Hill Holliday is the only woman in London who runs an advertising agency's creative department single-handed. She thinks agencies are aware of the problem, but blames incompetence rather than deliberate sexism.

Clients point to the fact that women still buy their products—a silly argument, since people who wash clothes will buy washing powder whether it is advertised or not. If a company advertised women's products really well, it would win market share from its competitors. A fortune could await the agency which can meet that need.

And she's the customer, now

Source: *The Economist,* January 17th, 1987.

Questions
(i) To what extent do television adverts target women successfully?
(ii) Why might advertising agencies begin looking more seriously at advertisements aimed at working women?
(iii) To what extent can advertising be considered socially wasteful?

(i) The article notes that the advertisements targeted at women who stay at home are widespread, although many women object to the stereotyped image which these contain. Advertisers are not so effective in getting rid of the old-fashioned image of women and targeting those working women with families, aged 25 to 44, who, as we are told, have £11.3 billion of income at their disposal.

(ii) Firstly, as already noted, these women have significant spending power. On top of that we are told that 15% of women who stay at home now plan to work in the future. Possibly even more significant is the prediction in the article that over the next few years mothers will have fewer children and go back to work more quickly after having their babies.

(iii) This question requires you to think beyond the article. But even in the article commercials for soap powders are mentioned. The market for soap powders is dominated by two firms. They are advertising against each other and even advertising their own brands against one another. Thus, much of the advertising might be regarded as mutually offsetting and therefore a waste of limited resources. In fact, most firms which find themselves in oligopolistic markets advertise heavily, which may indeed be socially wasteful.

EXERCISE

Read the following extract and answer the questions which follow it.

Untroubled on the factory floor

An intriguing footnote to the government's trade-union legislation is being written in Northern Ireland. New legislation often becomes law in mainland Britain before it affects Ulster. Now, the government has proposed that its 1982 Employment Act—whose main provisions allow unions to be sued, narrow the definition of a trade dispute and require closed shops to be supported by 85% of the workforce in a secret ballot—should be law in Northern Ireland.

The unions in the province are, not surprisingly, hostile. More surprising is the fact that there is also some wariness among employers. Despite (some say, because of) the sectarian troubles outside the factory gate, industrial relations in the province are good. Between October 1984 and September last year, industry on the mainland lost, on average, nearly 12 working days a month per 1,000 employees—even before the effects of the miners' strike are taken into account. The figure for Northern Ireland: fewer than five.

This comparative industrial harmony results largely from the small size of the province, and the employment structure itself: many Northern Irish companies are small, family-owned and paternalistic. The result is a system not so much like the modern one of employee involvement that is popular in Britain among Japanese and some American companies, and more like the atmosphere in, say, the coal mines before nationalisation, when the men went to the pit manager's house for garden parties, but doffed their caps to him in between. This old-fashioned friendliness might not last, if more modern companies took the bait of grants offered to them to locate in Northern Ireland.

So why the hostility to the proposed new laws on industrial relations? After all, the 1982 act need not itself make much difference: most of its provisions can be, and on the mainland often have been, ignored. Employers and unions are more worried about what might happen after the introduction of the more influential 1984 Trade Union Act, for which Northern Ireland secretary, Mr Tom King, was himself responsible. In mainland Britain, trade unions are beginning to appreciate, and employers to fear, that the requirement to ballot before strikes can sometimes strengthen the unions' bargaining hand.

In Northern Ireland, doubts about the act's usefulness have a more sinister origin. In most companies, Catholics and Protestants work harmoniously side by side. Trade-union leaders and some employers fear that industrial ballots would quickly become an excuse for division along sectarian lines, and thereby jeopardise their joint success in keeping the troubles off the factory floor.

Source: *The Economist*, May 17th, 1986.

Questions

(i) Outline the reasons why industrial relations in Northern Ireland seem to be better than they are on the mainland.

(ii) What are the advantages and disadvantages of closed shops?

E. HANDLING THE DATA-RESPONSE QUESTION

What is Expected of You?

Before looking at the way to tackle a data-response question, let us look at what you are expected to be able to do. The examination boards all have slightly different aims and objectives but most of them stress that you should be able to:
—handle, interpret and present statistical evidence;
—solve problems and make decisions based on the data provided;
—evaluate the reliability of data presented;
—understand the line of argument and confirm that any conclusions drawn in the text are consistent with the information given;
—discriminate between alternative explanations, evaluate arguments arising from the data and present alternatives where appropriate;
—apply appropriate theories which fit the data;
—translate data into technical economic terms;
—communicate your results effectively.

This may look rather daunting at first glance, so it is important that you practise your skills in this area. The following guidelines will help you to present a good answer. Keep them with you when you first begin to answer questions.

Tackling the Question

1. Do not rush into the question. Approach it in a systematic way.
2. Read all the material provided, and make sure you understand it.
3. Read the questions through carefully.
4. Consider the data in the light of the questions.
5. Select and underline the material contained in the question which is directly relevant to the question.
6. Pay particular attention to any conclusions drawn in the text and work out the main line of argument.
7. Consider what supporting material is needed in the answer.
8. Ask yourself what assumptions have been made in the material or what assumptions need to be made.
9. Ask yourself if the data can be supported by any particular theory.
10. Look for footnotes. These can provide clues as to the source of the data.

Once you have done this, underlining important points and making notes and comments in the margin, you are in a position to begin writing your answer.

Writing the Answer

1. Read the questions once again and remember that you must respond directly to them and not just summarise the data.
2. Do not describe everything in minute detail or reproduce the data exactly, as this defeats the object of the question.
3. Be selective in your answer, eliminating surplus material.
4. Make sure that your answer and your argument progress in a logical way. Structure is important.
5. Identify underlying relationships in the data and make clear the assumptions on which they are based.
6. Remember that there is no single correct answer. You should therefore exercise your judgement and argue points to a conclusion, identifying supporting material.

There are four things common in poor answers which you should aim to avoid:
   Inadequate preparation
   Superficiality
   Misdirection
   Irrelevance
By following the guide above you can avoid each of these.

'Too many candidates persist in merely paraphrasing the information or data given in the questions rather than interpreting or analysing. A significant proportion of candidates fail to apply basic economic concepts to appropriate situations.'
(University of London Examiners' Report: A Level Economics, June 1984.)

EXAMPLE 1

Profit sharing

A greater share in success

In his March budget, Mr Nigel Lawson, the chancellor of the exchequer, announced new income-tax incentives to encourage companies to introduce profit-related pay (PRP). Since Mr Lawson first mooted the idea a year ago, all sorts of claims have been made about the benefits of profit sharing. Now a new study* provides a comprehensive round-up of the theory and facts.

The theory
Three advantages are claimed for PRP:
● It gives workers a stake in the success of a firm. This should improve industrial relations, encourage employees to work harder, and so boost productivity.
● It makes wages more flexible and hence employment more stable. In a recession, wages will fall and so fewer workers will lose their jobs.
● It will reduce unemployment. It is this bold claim, based on the work of Professor Martin Weitzman, which has generated much of the recent interest in PRP.

Mr Weitzman's theory is persuasive. If a firm pays each of its workers wages of £200 a week, it will employ people up to the point where the extra revenue generated by an additional worker is exactly equal to £200. Average revenue per worker might be, say, £300, to cover overheads and profit.

Suppose that the firm then decides to switch to PRP, paying a basic wage of £160 a week, plus a share of profits. To leave the worker as well off as before, this share would need initially to be £40. That is two-sevenths of the firm's profits per worker, which will now be £140—ie, £300 minus £160.

The firm now has a big incentive to hire extra labour. The marginal revenue to be earned from taking on an extra worker is still £200, but the marginal cost is only £160 plus two-sevenths of the extra profit (£200 minus £160), ie, £171.43. PRP has reduced the cost of employing new workers, and so more will be employed.

The snag is that if a firm adopts PRP, existing workers will be made worse off when new workers are recruited, as this will dilute their share of total profits. Is

profit sharing not just a fancy way of cutting pay?

Mr Weitzman agrees that for an individual firm, new recruitment will cut average pay; but if all firms adopt PRP, the higher demand for labour will push up real wages and everybody will be better off. In other words, there exists what economists call an "externality". If this is so, there is a strong case for a tax subsidy to encourage more firms to adopt PRP.

Participation pays

Firms in the UK metal-working industry, 1982

	Non-profit-sharing	Profit-sharing
Working days lost due to strikes (per employee)	13.1	8.4
Turnover rates %		
unskilled	4.65	3.83
skilled	4.34	3.51
Percentage of labour force unionised	72.0	87.8
Value added per worker	10.2	10.9
Value added per unit of fixed assets	2.9	3.7
Rate of return on capital employed %	−1.7	13.7

Source: Estrin and Wilson (1986)

If PRP is to reduce unemployment, two conditions must be fulfilled. First, the firm must count only the basic wage as the marginal cost of hiring an extra person. If employers still focus on total remuneration—because, for example, they feel they have to pay the going rate to retain skilled workers—PRP will make no difference to employment.

Second, if it is to create jobs, PRP must reduce average labour costs. That may happen in one of two ways. Either—as Mr Weitzman assumes—employees will accept a fall in profit-linked income, and not insist on a higher basic wage as compensation. Or productivity may rise.

The facts
A careful sifting of the various studies on profit sharing fails to provide any evidence that the firm treats only the basic wage as the marginal cost. Firms still seem to think in terms of total remuneration. However, there is some evidence

that PRP reduces total pay per worker, and that it boosts employment.

One study† examined a sample of 52 medium-sized firms in the engineering and metal-working industries over the period 1978-82. Four in ten of the firms had some sort of profit sharing. The results: average total pay (including profit share) was 4% lower in profit-sharing firms than in non-profit-sharing ones, and PRP seemed to increase employment by an average of 13%. However, the authors concluded that only 0.5% of the extra employment was due to Weitzman-type effects; most was probably attributable to higher productivity.

Several studies confirm that PRP improves a company's productivity. The Estrin-Wilson paper found that companies with profit sharing had 50% fewer strikes and significantly lower labour turnover (see table). The average productivity of labour was only slightly higher, but capital productivity was on average 25% higher. Moreover, profit-sharing firms achieved an average return on capital of 14%; the others had negative returns averaging almost 2%.

It is hard to be sure whether productivity is higher because of PRP, or because good managers are more likely to introduce PRP. Anyway, the spur for workers in firms with PRP seems to be not the incentive of bonuses, but the greater

sense of participation they enjoy. Yet Mr Weitzman's argument requires that workers be kept out of management, to stop them resisting the hiring of new workers. So the two main motives behind profit sharing conflict. If workers are given a say in the running of the company, few jobs will be created; if they are excluded from decision-making, the potential gains in productivity may be thrown away.

If the main effect of PRP is not to increase jobs, but to boost productivity—and thus profits—then why should companies be bribed with tax relief to adopt it? If PRP is really just about motivating people to work harder, then the government's new tax incentives may not be the best way of going about it. It might be more effective to relate pay to an individual's effort rather than to the whole company's performance. The optimal incentive scheme would depend on factors such as the size of the company, the production process and the product, but the choice should be left to the firm. The government's proposed tax incentive will distort that choice.

The Economist, April 25th, 1987.

* Profit sharing and employee share ownership, by Saul Estrin, Paul Grout, and Sushil Wadhwani. Economic Policy, April 1987
† The microeconomic effects of profit sharing: the British experience. S. Estrin and N. Wilson. Centre for Labour Economics

Questions:

 (i) Explain the first two of the three advantages claimed for profit-sharing in terms of economic theory.

(ii) It is claimed that profit-sharing will enable wages to fall in certain circumstances. Explain why firms may be reluctant to see this happen.

(iii) Discuss advantages and disadvantages of linking together profit-sharing and worker participation in the management of the firm.

Stage 1: tackling the questions
Having read through the article once and looked carefully at the questions, it can be useful to look at the article again, underlining the sections which will be of direct use in your answers.

Profit sharing

A greater share in success

In his March budget, Mr Nigel Lawson, the chancellor of the exchequer, announced new income-tax incentives to encourage companies to introduce profit-related pay (PRP). Since Mr Lawson first mooted the idea a year ago, all sorts of claims have been made about the benefits of profit sharing. Now a new study* provides a comprehensive round-up of the theory and facts.

The theory
Three advantages are claimed for PRP:
● It gives workers a stake in the success of a firm. This should improve industrial relations, encourage employees to work harder, and so boost productivity.
● It makes wages more flexible and hence employment more stable. In a recession, wages will fall and so fewer workers will lose their jobs.
● It will reduce unemployment. It is this bold claim, based on the work of Professor Martin Weitzman, which has generated much of the recent interest in PRP.

Mr Weitzman's theory is persuasive. If a firm pays each of its workers wages of £200 a week, it will employ people up to the point where the extra revenue generated by an additional worker is exactly equal to £200. Average revenue per worker might be, say, £300, to cover overheads and profit.

Suppose that the firm then decides to switch to PRP, paying a basic wage of £160 a week, plus a share of profits. To leave the worker as well off as before, this share would need initially to be £40. That is two-sevenths of the firm's profits per worker, which will now be £140—ie, £300 minus £160.

The firm now has a big incentive to hire extra labour. The marginal revenue to be earned from taking on an extra worker is still £200, but the marginal cost is only £160 plus two-sevenths of the extra profit (£200 minus £160), ie, £171.43. PRP has reduced the cost of employing new workers, and so more will be employed.

The snag is that if a firm adopts PRP, existing workers will be made worse off when new workers are recruited, as this will dilute their share of total profits. Is profit sharing not just a fancy way of cutting pay?

Mr Weitzman agrees that for an individual firm, new recruitment will cut average pay; but if all firms adopt PRP, the higher demand for labour will push up real wages and everybody will be better off. In other words, there exists what economists call an "externality". If this is so, there is a strong case for a tax subsidy to encourage more firms to adopt PRP.

Participation pays

Firms in the UK metal-working industry, 1982

	Non-profit-sharing	Profit-sharing
Working days lost due to strikes (per employee)	13.1	8.4
Turnover rates %		
unskilled	4.65	3.83
skilled	4.34	3.51
Percentage of labour force unionised	72.0	87.8
Value added per worker	10.2	10.9
Value added per unit of fixed assets	2.9	3.7
Rate of return on capital employed %	−1.7	13.7

Source: Estrin and Wilson (1986)

If PRP is to reduce unemployment, two conditions must be fulfilled. First, the firm must count only the basic wage as the marginal cost of hiring an extra person. If employers still focus on total remuneration—because, for example, they feel they have to pay the going rate to retain skilled workers—PRP will make no difference to employment.

Second, if it is to create jobs, PRP must reduce average labour costs. That may happen in one of two ways. Either—as Mr Weitzman assumes—employees will accept a fall in profit-linked income, and not insist on a higher basic wage as compensation. Or productivity may rise.

The facts
A careful sifting of the various studies on profit sharing fails to provide any evidence that the firm treats only the basic wage as the marginal cost. Firms still seem to think in terms of total remuneration. However, there is some evidence

that PRP reduces total pay per worker, and that it boosts employment.

One study† examined a sample of 52 medium-sized firms in the engineering and metal-working industries over the period 1978-82. Four in ten of the firms had some sort of profit sharing. The results: average total pay (including profit share) was 4% lower in profit-sharing firms than in non-profit-sharing ones, and PRP seemed to increase employment by an average of 13%. However, the authors concluded that only 0.5% of the extra employment was due to Weitzman-type effects; most was probably attributable to higher productivity.

Several studies confirm that PRP improves a company's productivity. The Estrin-Wilson paper found that companies with profit sharing had 50% fewer strikes and significantly lower labour turnover (see table). The average productivity of labour was only slightly higher, but capital productivity was on average 25% higher. Moreover, profit-sharing firms achieved an average return on capital of 14%; the others had negative returns averaging almost 2%.

It is hard to be sure whether productivity is higher because of PRP, or because good managers are more likely to introduce PRP. Anyway, the spur for workers in firms with PRP seems to be not the incentive of bonuses, but the greater sense of participation they enjoy. Yet Mr Weitzman's argument requires that workers be kept out of management, to stop them resisting the hiring of new workers. So the two main motives behind profit sharing conflict. If workers are given a say in the running of the company, few jobs will be created; if they are excluded from decision-making, the potential gains in productivity may be thrown away.

If the main effect of PRP is not to increase jobs, but to boost productivity—and thus profits—then why should companies be bribed with tax relief to adopt it? If PRP is really just about motivating people to work harder, then the government's new tax incentives may not be the best way of going about it. It might be more effective to relate pay to an individual's effort rather than to the whole company's performance. The optimal incentive scheme would depend on factors such as the size of the company, the production process and the product, but the choice should be left to the firm. The government's proposed tax incentive will distort that choice.

* Profit sharing and employee share ownership, by Saul Estrin, Paul Grout, and Sushil Wadhwani. Economic Policy, April 1987
† The microeconomic effects of profit sharing: the British experience. S. Estrin and N. Wilson. Centre for Labour Economics

Stage 2: writing the answer

Tackle each question in turn, using the article to reinforce the points you wish to make. Here are the bare bones around which you should build a well-rounded answer:

(i) The first advantage is associated with boosts in productivity as a result of improved industrial relations. This can be seen as a shift in the average product of labour as illustrated in the diagram below:

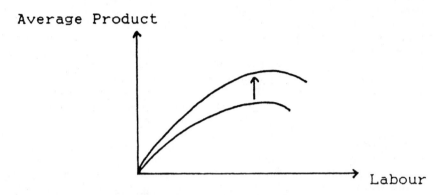

The second advantage is associated with making wages flexible downwards. Thus, if we are faced with a recession and the demand for a firm's product falls, then because labour is a derived demand, so too, will the demand for labour. Suppose demand for labour falls from D to D^1. If wages remained the same, this would create unemployment L1–L2. But if wages fall from W1 to W2 then fewer people (L1–L3) lose their jobs.

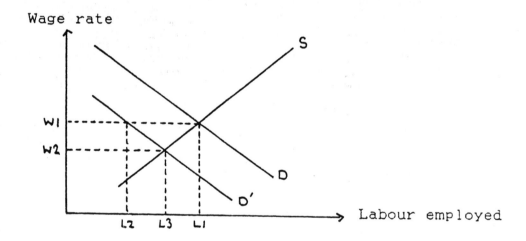

(ii) As the article suggests, firms may feel that 'they have to pay the going rate to retain skilled workers'. Thus, if wages were to fall in a firm which in one year did not make a profit, its skilled workers would move to another firm. The original firm would then have an even worse problem to contend with. On the other hand, the article does note many aspects which may encourage the firm to adopt a profit-sharing scheme. These include greater productivity and fewer strikes.

(iii) As the article points out, 'the two main motives behind profit-sharing conflict'.

On the one hand, workers should not be allowed to have a say in the management of the firm, since they will want to prevent the recruitment of new staff, because this dilutes their share of profits. But if tax benefits for those accepting PRP were to be introduced, these feelings might be mitigated. On the other hand, many of the benefits associated with profit-sharing stem from improved industrial relations and these could be further enhanced by participation in management.

The article does point out that where employment did increase, the dominant factor seemed to be productivity influences rather than the Weitzman-type effects. On reflection then, it might be the improved industrial relations part of the formula which should be emphasised and participation therefore increased.

EXAMPLE 2

Below is a set of statistics relating to the population and gross domestic product of three countries. Study the figures carefully and answer the following questions:

	Country 1		Country 2		Country 3	
Population ('000)	1987	2000 (projected)	1987	2000 (projected)	1987	2000 (projected)
Under 13 years old	23,221	22,362	3,271	3,635	17,231	20,470
14–21 years old	16,947	16,921	2,317	3,326	15,361	16,390
22–44 years old	33,250	27,860	5,276	2,945	14,271	15,900
45–64 years old	22,920	23,250	2,311	4,991	9,333	15,630
65+	11,876	17,331	1,261	1,914	1,262	1,290
Total	108,214	107,724	14,436	16,811	57,458	69,680
Gross domestic product £bn (1987) (GDP)	421.8		16.1		14.2	

Questions:

(i) Briefly assess each country's stage of development and standard of living. Give reasons for your assessment.

(ii) Discuss the usefulness of the gross domestic product measure as an indicator of standard of living.

(i) Before examining each country in turn, we need to consider whether the table provides us with adequate information to enable us to answer the question. The only measure of standard of living that we will be able to examine is per capita gross domestic product. It will be useful, therefore, to work out the figures for each country. This is done by dividing GDP by population. This yields the following results:

        Country 1 £3,897
        Country 2 £1,115
        Country 3 £247

Now go on to look at each country in turn:

Country 1

This country has a very large population and a large GDP. It has the highest standard of living (measured by per capita GDP) of all the three countries. From the population figures we see that a decline is expected into the year 2000. But note that the number of over 65s is predicted to rise quite dramatically. We can assume that health care must be improving significantly for this age group. We must assume, therefore, that this is an established industralised country with a population approximately double that of the U.K.

Country 2

This country has the second highest standard of living. Its population is significantly smaller than those of the other countries and predicted to rise to a limited extent over the next two decades. If we are assuming the first country to be an established industrialised one, then perhaps this is a newly-industrialised country. Certainly its GDP per capita figure would seem to indicate that this could be the case.

Country 3

This country has a very low standard of living with only £247 GDP per head. Its population is projected to expand quite rapidly, but not in the older age group, which we highlighted before as being a sign of better health care. Note in particular the increase in the under 13 age group. One can only assume this to be a Third World country.

General points to think about:

We can only make rough guesses at the sorts of countries these are. We are using the limited information available, together with our knowledge of trends in the differing countries, to come to a tentative conclusion. It would be worth mentioning in any answer that additional information would be required before we could come to definite conclusions.

(ii) The measure of GDP is not the most reliable way to measure standard of living, because it leaves out many factors which may be important. Omission of these can result in either overstatement or understatement of the true level of GDP. For example:

—No account is taken of pollution, which can adversely affect people's standard of living.

—Not all transactions in an economy are recorded. This is particularly true in less-developed countries. The unrecorded transactions are often referred to as the Black Economy.

EXERCISE 1

House prices

Ever upwards

Spring is here: would-be home-buyers have come out of their winter hibernation and are pushing house prices ever higher. In 1986, the average price of a home in Britain rose by about 11%—almost four times the rate of inflation. As the year drew to a close, most people predicted that the pace of increase would slow during 1987. Instead, it seems to be accelerating.

According to the Nationwide Building Society, average prices rose 17% in the 12 months to the January-March quarter, and by as much as 27% in London. The Nationwide predicts that the average rate of increase could reach 20% by the end of the year—a real increase of around 15%. Five factors appear to be fuelling the boom:

● The strongest is the rapid rise in real personal disposable income. Earnings are still outpacing retail prices, and the latest income-tax cuts will put more money into people's pockets.

● It has never been easier to borrow money to buy a house. Banks and building societies are often lending 100% of the value of a property, and four or even five times the borrower's income.

● The recent drop in mortgage-interest rates—and the hope of more to come—should help to boost demand. The lower the rate of interest, the more a house buyer can afford to borrow. Real interest rates, however, are still high in relation to the early 1970s. The mortgage repayments of the average first-time buyer are 10% higher as a percentage of income than at the peak of the 1973 boom.

● The baby boom of the 1960s is now pushing up the demand for housing. During the five years to 1991, the number of households in Britain is forecast to rise by an average of 170,000 a year—the biggest increase since the 1960s. Then, later in the 1990s, demography should tend to depress the market: the number of households is expected to rise by only 55,000 a year in the second half of the decade.

● Home ownership is more than just a roof over one's head; it is also an investment. The rapid rise in prices, especially in London and the south-east, has encouraged home buyers to borrow more and trade up in anticipation of a bigger capital gain. The bigger the speculative element in this boom, the bigger the risk of a crash.

In West Germany and Belgium, and on the west coast of America, house prices have tumbled in recent years. Could the same happen in Britain? At present, probably not. The countries with falling prices all have larger private-rental markets, which allow people to move in and out of the owner-occupied market with ease.

In Britain most people have little alternative to buying a house. Thanks to rent controls, the private-rental sector has shrunk from almost half of the total housing stock in 1950 to less than 10% today, while it is still up at 60% in West Germany. So British home-owners cannot easily sell up and rent. This helps to explain why in Britain, unlike in other countries, house prices in cash terms have risen in each of the past 35 years. (In real terms, by contrast, prices dropped 36% in the four years to 1977, and only regained their 1973 level last year.)

How long will the fast rise in prices continue? The ratio of house prices to average earnings may provide a clue. At a national level, the ratio is only just above its long-term average of 3.5. It is still well below the peaks of 4.95 in 1973 and 3.82 in 1979, suggesting that there is plenty of room for further increases.

But the national figures are somewhat

misleading; since 1983, house prices have risen by 83% in London—three times as much as in the rest of the country. In London and the south-east, the ratio of house prices to earnings reached 4.5 last year (see chart).   If London house prices continue to rise at their current pace, then the price-earnings ratio will pass its 1973 peak of 5.6 around the end of this year. The higher prices climb, the more first-time buyers will be priced out—they are already having to fork out at least £50,000 to get on to the first rung of the London housing ladder. London's house-price boom may not have much further to run.

Outside Britain's south-east, the ratio of house prices to earnings has hardly budged in recent years. At just over 3, it is well below its level in the early 1970s. The gap between house prices in the north and south of Britain has never been greater. The price of the average house in London is now 126% more than in north-west England, compared with an average premium of only 50% in the ten years to 1983. How long before a luxury kennel in London fetches more than a Bradford semi?

The obvious reason for the widening gap is the greater prosperity and lower unemployment in the south, reinforced by demographic pressures. The Department of the Environment predicts that the number of households in the south-east will grow by 11% in the 15 years to 2001, but by only 4% in the north.

However, it is not only in London where house prices have taken off this year. According to the Halifax Building Society, prices are growing more rapidly this year than last in all regions except the north-west. Prices have risen by 10% or more in Yorkshire and Humberside, the Midlands, East Anglia, Wales and the south-west. That, in turn, should give a boost to the construction industry. Britain's economic recovery may be spreading northwards at last.

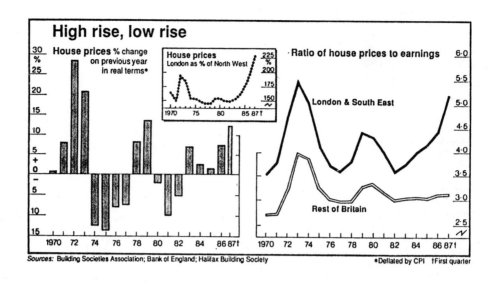

High rise, low rise

House prices % change on previous year in real terms*

House prices London as % of North West

Ratio of house prices to earnings

London & South East

Rest of Britain

Sources: Building Societies Association; Bank of England; Halifax Building Society

*Deflated by CPI   †First quarter

The Economist, April 18, 1987

Questions

(i) Using the passage on p.111 and the graph which accompanies it (above), outline the factors which indicate that house prices will continue to rise.

(ii) Using economic theory, demonstrate why house prices are higher in London and the South-East than in the rest of Britain.

(iii) Outline what you consider to be a likely trend in house prices over the next decade. Give reasons for your analysis.

HINTS

(i) These factors are contained both in the text and in the graphs provided. In the graphs, note the upward trends, particularly in London and the South-East. In the text, five factors are highlighted in the first column, which are said to be 'fuelling the boom'; there are also a couple of factors elsewhere in the text.

(ii) Reading through the text, it should be obvious that the rapid rise in house prices in the South is a simple matter of supply not being sufficient for the demand. Construct a sensible supply and demand diagram to show this.

(iii) This is a matter for your own analysis. Some suggestions are given in the text with which you can choose to agree or disagree. Remember, though, that whatever 'side' you choose to come down on, your answer must be well argued and structured.

EXERCISE 2

What Brazil can learn from Bolivia

Since the beginning of 1985, three Latin American countries have tried to curb their high inflation. Bolivia's programme has succeeded, at a cost. Argentina's is starting to slip. Brazil's has collapsed

The economists who devised the three anti-inflation packages—Bolivia's blandly titled New Economic Policy (NEP), Argentina's Austral plan, and Brazil's Cruzado plan—consciously set out to test two rival theories of inflation. The Austral and Cruzado plans were based on the idea that high inflation sustains itself. Because of this "inertia", cutting inflation by squeezing monetary and fiscal policy will prove costly in lost output and unemployment; a temporary prices-and-incomes policy is needed to snap the economy back to stable prices. Bolivia's NEP was based on the opposite view: inflation has no built-in momentum of its own, and can be halted by a decisive change in monetary and fiscal policy.

Argentina's Austral plan, announced in July 1985, was the first. President Raul Alfonsin's government froze prices and wages, created a new currency—the austral—and tied its value to the dollar. By April 1986, the government had to retreat. Its price controls were starting to slip, and the unions were complaining about the fall in real incomes. Wages and prices were allowed to rise faster, forcing a series of devaluations. In September 1986, the government reimposed its wage controls, but the intention this time was to keep wage increases low, rather than to ban them altogether.

The revised plan worked well—initially. Argentina's inflation rate tumbled (see chart). But by the end of last year, it was going up again. The most recent inflation figures (for January 1987) showed a worrying rise in the monthly rate. At the end of February, to howls of protest, the government slapped on a new wages-and-prices freeze.

Brazil's anti-inflation plan was modelled on Argentina's: price and wage controls, a new currency (the cruzado), an exchange-rate freeze. By the time it

came into effect, in February 1986, the Austral plan was doing so well that Brazil's President José Sarney, was confident. His speeches parroted the "inertia" view of inflation: prices had been knocked upwards by a series of economic shocks; fiscal policy was not to blame; a prices-and-incomes policy would stop inflation at a stroke.

Within nine months, Brazil's economy had become a classic case of repressed inflation: demand kept rising, prices soared on black markets, queues and shortages appeared everywhere. By the time of last November's congressional elections, the plan had lost all credibility. Since then, it has collapsed.

Why did the Cruzado plan crumble so much faster than the similar-looking Austral plan? Mr Sarney made a big mistake in sweetening his price-and-wage freeze with an 8-15% wage hike. That stoked demand. Another mistake was to wind up the state's index-linked savings scheme; a lot of that money fled into black-market dollars, driving down the cruzado. Above all, though, Brazil failed to tackle its public-sector deficit. At first, Mr Sarney expected it to be 0.5% of GDP in 1986. When that forecast began to go wrong, he took no decisive action. The deficit was probably more than 5% of GDP.

Bolivia's NEP took an altogether different tack. The government announced a tight monetary and fiscal squeeze; its budget deficit fell from 28% of GDP in 1984 to 4% of GDP in 1986. It devalued the Bolivian peso by a massive 90%, then let it float in a daily dollar auction. Inflation fell from an annual rate of more than 20,000% in 1985 to 10% in the second half of 1986.

This stunning fall in Bolivia's inflation was achieved without resort to the price controls that were a central feature of

the Austral and Cruzado plans. A recent issue of the IMF's newsletter drools over Bolivia's success. The NEP was much closer than either of the other plans to the orthodox anti-inflation policies that the Fund typically recommends. Brazil's economic planners are squirming. For them, one of the biggest advantages of the Cruzado plan was that it would teach the IMF that fiscal austerity is not the way to cut inflation. It hasn't.

The collapse of the Cruzado plan confirms the importance of fiscal policy, but it has not settled the debate over prices-and-incomes policies. Some economists argue that, if combined with a tight fiscal policy, temporary wage-and-price controls can help to cut inflation down less painfully. They say that Bolivia, despite its anti-inflation success, is in the midst of a fearful recession—though this was well underway before the NEP, and now seems to be moderating. (Bolivia's GDP fell by 2.9% in 1986, compared with a 4.1% fall in 1985.)

The last hope of advocates of a kindly escape from hyperinflation is on the other side of the world. **Israel's** anti-inflation plan, begun in 1985, combined wage-and-price controls with big cuts in the government's budget deficit. It brought down inflation, which was reaching an annual rate of 1,000% just before the 1985 freeze, to around 20% during 1986. The budget deficit has dropped from over 10% of GDP in 1985 to around 3% in 1986, although Israel's real government expenditure is still rising; the improvement has come because taxes are now being paid in real money, instead of everybody trying to wait a year in a 1,000% inflation to pay taxes at 0.1 cents on the dollar. The worst slippage has been in wages, which have outpaced prices, so that real private consumption rose by 10½% in 1986, and civilian imports have soared. This is not what the formulators of Israel's plan intended, but it is nothing like a Cruzado crisis yet.

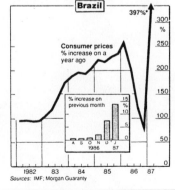

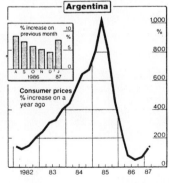

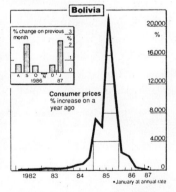

The Economist, March 14, 1987

Questions

(i) After reading the article, assess the importance of the following policies as a means of reducing inflation in South America:

(a) prices and incomes policies;

(b) a tight monetary and fiscal policy.

(ii) To what extent have these policies been used successfully in the U.K. economy in the past two decades?

F. CHECKLIST √   √   √   √   √   √   √   √   √   √   √

1	Do not be misled by statistics or the presentation of data.
2	There are many sources of data available. Try to use some of these in your studies.
3	Think about the application of economic theory when handling data.
4	Look for trends and relationships in statistical data, but do not assume a direction of causation.
5	Always study data thoroughly and critically, so as not to miss important points.
6	Do not rush into tackling data-response questions. Careful preparation is needed.
7	Consider the data in the light of the questions. Underline important points.
8	Be selective when writing your answer. Use the data provided to support your points.
9	Avoid irrelevance and superficiality in your answer.
10	Remember that there is no single correct answer.

G. END OF CHAPTER EXERCISES

EXERCISE 1

LLOYDS BANK ECONOMIC BULLETIN

A MONTHLY ANALYSIS FROM LLOYDS BANK   NUMBER 110   FEBRUARY 1988

The recovery lurches on

The UK's rate of real economic growth in 1987 was just over 4 per cent, higher than in any other industrial country except Spain. Such an increase in gdp is, however, by no means unusual in British post-war economic history. The economy has grown by 4 per cent or more in 7 previous years since 1948, most recently by 7.3 per cent in 1973. The problem is that it has hardly ever been possible to maintain such a high rate of growth for more than one year. It looks as if 1987 will be no exception, with gdp officially forecast to increase by 2½ per cent in 1988.

The growth of gdp (gross domestic product) is in fact difficult to measure accurately. The three different methods used in the UK are based on net output (value added), expenditure and income. In theory gdp (O), gdp (E) and gdp (I) should all show the same rate of growth, since they are by definition equal to each other. In practice they diverge, so for most purposes an average of the three is taken, called gdp (A).

Chart A shows the main constituents of each measure of gdp. Errors of measurement in any of them will result in an inaccurate gdp statistic. Gdp (O) is often the most reliable measure in the short run, because it is usually less in need of subsequent upwards revision than the two other measures. In recent years it has been growing faster as well. Gdp (I) has been growing as rapidly as gdp (O), while gdp (E) has been growing more slowly. In the 1970s, income was apparently being underestimated relative to expenditure, because of the

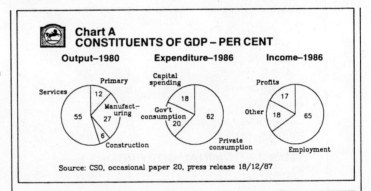

Chart A
CONSTITUENTS OF GDP – PER CENT

Output–1980   Expenditure–1986   Income–1986

Source: CSO, occasional paper 20, press release 18/12/87

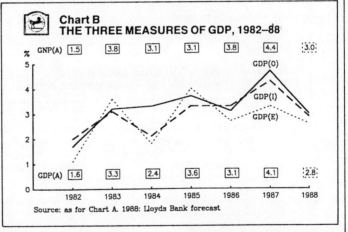

Chart B
THE THREE MEASURES OF GDP, 1982–88

% GNP(A) 1.5 3.8 3.1 3.1 3.8 4.4 3.0

GDP(A) 1.6 3.3 2.4 3.6 3.1 4.1 2.8

Source: as for Chart A. 1988: Lloyds Bank forecast

'black economy', but in the 1980s expenditure has been underestimated even more than income. For example, both capital investment and invisible exports are likely not to have been fully recorded in the official figures. Since 1981 an allowance of no more than 1¼ per cent has been made for an income shortfall due to tax evasion, even though it is likely that the true figure is higher.

Chart B shows how far apart the three measures of gdp growth are in each year. Gdp (E) shows a particularly bumpy pattern, actually exceeding the other measures in some years, but more often undershooting them. The average measure, gdp (A), also tends to rise and fall in alternate years. This is partly due to the coal strike in 1984, which would otherwise have been another year of 4

ANALYSIS OF GROWTH OF GROSS DOMESTIC PRODUCT
A = Percentage annual increases   B = Contributions to GDP growth

Table 1 – REAL GDP (OUTPUT)

	1981-87 A	1981-87 B	1987 A	1987 B	1988 A	1988 B
Agriculture	1.6	0.03	−0.9	−0.02	0.0	0.0
Energy & water	3.1	0.3	−3.0	−0.3	−5.0	−0.5
Manufacturing	1.4	0.4	5.7	1.5	3.5	0.9
Construction	1.4	0.1	8.4	0.5	4.0	0.2
Services	3.2	1.8	5.6	3.0	4.4	2.4
Real gdp (0)	2.6	2.6	4.7	4.7	3.0	3.0

Table 2 – REAL GDP (EXPENDITURE)

	1981-87 A	1981-87 B	1987 A	1987 B	1988 A	1988 B
Consumers' expenditure	3.1	1.9	4.8	3.0	4.0	2.5
General government expenditure	0.7	0.2	0.0	0.0	1.0	0.2
Fixed investment	2.1	0.4	3.4	0.6	4.0	0.7
Change in stockbuilding†	0.2	0.2	0.0	0.0	0.0	0.0
Domestic demand	2.7	2.7	3.6	3.6	3.4	3.4
Exports of goods and services	3.5	1.0	6.9	2.0	2.5	0.7
Imports of goods and services	4.9	−1.4	7.9	−2.3	5.5	−1.5
Foreign balance†	−0.4	−0.4	−0.3	−0.3	−0.8	−0.8
Real gdp (E)	2.3	2.3	3.3	3.3	2.6	2.6
Compromise adjustment†	0.2	0.2	0.8	0.8	0.2	0.2
Real gdp (A)	2.5	2.5	4.1	4.1	2.8	2.8

Table 3 – NOMINAL GDP (INCOME)

	1981-87 A	1981-87 B	1987 A	1987 B	1988 A	1988 B
Employment	7.3	5.0	7.6	4.9	8.0	5.2
Other	9.4	1.6	10.3	1.8	8.0	1.4
Gross trading profits*	12.3	1.7	12.2	2.1	8.0	1.4
Nominal gdp (I)	8.3	8.3	8.8	8.8	8.0	8.0
Real gdp (I)	2.6		4.3		2.9	

†As per cent of gdp   *Net of stock appreciation.
Source: CSO Press release, 18 December 1987. Lloyds Bank estimates and forecasts.

per cent growth; the pattern would in that case have been one of two peaks, in 1984 and 1987, rather than three, in 1983, 1985 and 1987.

The average rate of growth of gdp (A) was 2.5 per cent in 1981-87. That of gnp (gross national product) was 2.7 per cent, because net invisible income on the UK's net overseas assets – which enters into gnp but not gdp – was rising, from a small base in 1981, by 25 per cent a year in real terms. However, the UK population is growing at just over 0.1 per cent a year, so the increase in gnp per head differs hardly at all from that of total gdp, which may be taken as a fair indicator of economic growth.

Lloyds Bank Economic Bulletin, Number 110, February, 1988.

Read the extract above carefully, then answer the following questions:

1. What is meant by the 'black economy'?

2. What reasons other than the presence of a 'black economy' may account for discrepancies in the three measures of GDP?

3. Using the constituents of each measure of GDP, comment on where the growth in GDP has come from.

Study the diagram below and answer the following questions:

1. The diagram represents a 'natural monopoly'. What do the curves A, B and C represent?
   Why does the firm make a loss?

2. Explain why the existence of a natural monopoly is a strong argument in favour of nationalisation.

3. In practice, how can a firm in the situation portrayed below avoid a loss?

4. Show, with the aid of a diagram, how a monopolist able perfectly to price-discriminate will make maximum profits.

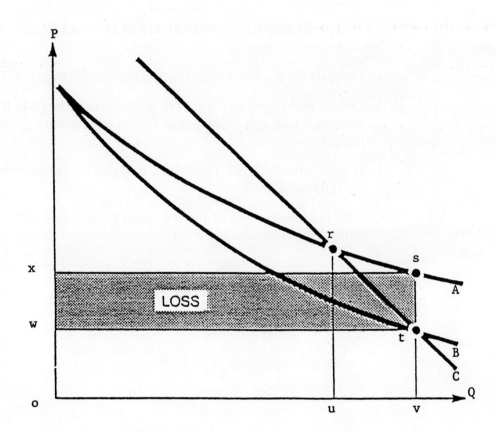

Table 1
LIVING STANDARDS IN MAJOR COUNTRIES
Gross domestic product per head at 1980 prices and purchasing power parities (rankings out of 6 countries in brackets)

	1960 % of USA	1970 % of USA	Increase % since 1960	1979 % of USA	Increase % since 1970	% of USA	1986 Increase % since 1979	1986 % since 1960	Level in current PPP$*
UK	66 (2)	64 (3)	24	66 (4)	22	66 (5)	9	66	11400
USA	100 (1)	100 (1)	27	100 (1)	19	100 (1)	9	65	17200
Japan	28 (6)	55 (5)	145	62 (5)	34	71 (3)	25	310	12200
Germany	60 (3)	67 (2)	42	72 (2)	27	74 (2)	13	104	12900
France	51 (4)	62 (4)	55	70 (3)	34	69 (4)	6	119	11800
Italy	42 (5)	54 (6)	63	57 (6)	25	57 (6)	10	124	9900

* USA in US dollars. Others converted into US dollars at PPP exchange rates.   Source: Eurostat, OECD.

Lloyds Bank Economic Bulletin, Number 100, April 1987

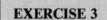
EXERCISE 3

Carefully examine tables 1 (above) and 2 (p.119 and 120) and answer the questions which follow:

1. Compare the growth in real domestic product between the U.K. and the U.S.A.

2. Compare and contrast the growth in productivity in the U.K. with that of other countries. Can you explain why British productivity growth ranks relatively highly?

3. In comparison with other countries, how well has the government done in bringing inflation down?

4. How did membership of the European Community (EC) affect U.K. prices? How can this be accounted for?

 **Table 2**
REAL GDP GROWTH 1960-86
At constant market prices. Per cent a year (rankings out of 12 countries in brackets)

A. By time periods

	1960-69	1970-79	1980-86	1982-86	1960-86
UK	3.1 (12)	2.4 (11)	1.4 (8=)	2.6 (3)	2.4 (12)
USA	3.9 (11)	2.7 (9)	2.1 (3)	2.5 (4)	3.0 (10)
Japan	10.1 (1)	5.1 (1)	3.8 (1)	3.6 (1)	6.6 (1)
EC	–	3.3	1.4	1.8	–
OECD	–	3.3	2.1	2.4	–

B. By administrations

	1960-64	1965-70	1971-74	1975-79	1980-86
UK	3.6 (12)	2.5 (12)	2.9 (9=)	2.0 (10)	1.4 (8=)
USA	3.7 (11)	3.4 (11)	2.9 (9=)	3.1 (4=)	2.1 (3)
Japan	10.1 (1)	10.0 (1)	4.7 (2=)	4.6 (2)	3.8 (1)
EC	–	4.5	3.9	2.5	1.4
OECD	–	4.7	3.7	3.0	2.1

C. Before and after EC membership

	1960-72	1973-86	1973-86 (UK outside EC)
UK	2.9	1.9	1.3
EC	5.1	2.2	2.3
UK as % of EC	57.0%	82.0%	57.0%

OUTPUT PER PERSON EMPLOYED 1970-86
Whole economy (rankings out of 12 countries in brackets)

By time periods

	1971-74	1975-79	1980-86	1982-86
UK	2.5 (8)	1.8 (6=)	1.8 (3=)	2.4 (2)
USA	1.0 (12)	0.8 (9)	0.7 (10=)	0.6 (12)
Japan	4.1 (1=)	3.6 (1)	2.8 (1)	2.7 (1)
EC	3.5	2.5	1.6	1.9
OECD	2.7	2.0	1.5	1.7

UNEMPLOYMENT 1960-86
**Per cent of labour force. ILO common definitions. Averages
(rankings out of 12 countries in brackets)**

A. By time periods

	1960-69	1970-79	1980-86	1982-86	1960-86
UK	1.9 (4)	4.3 (7)	10.6 (10)	11.7 (10)	5.1 (4)
USA	4.8 (6)	6.1 (9)	7.8 (4)	8.1 (4)	6.1 (6)
Japan	1.3 (3)	1.7 (2)	2.5 (2)	2.6 (2)	1.7 (2)
EC	–	4.2	9.9	11.0	–
OECD	–	4.2	7.5	8.1	–

B. By administrations

	1960-64	1965-70	1971-74	1975-79	1980-86
UK	1.8 (4)	2.2 (4)	3.4 (8)	5.4 (6)	10.6 (10)
USA	5.7 (7)	4.0 (6)	5.4 (9)	6.9 (9)	7.8 (4)
Japan	1.4 (3)	1.2 (3)	1.3 (3)	2.0 (2)	2.5 (2)
EC	–	–	3.3	5.3	9.9
OECD	–	–	3.5	5.1	7.5

continued

Handling Data continued

CONSUMER PRICE INFLATION
Per cent a year (rankings out of 12 countries in brackets)

A. By time periods

	1960-69	1970-79	1980-86	1982-86	1960-86
UK	3.6 (6)	12.5 (11)	8.1 (9)	5.5 (6)	8.0 (10)
USA	2.3 (1)	7.1 (3=)	6.1 (5=)	3.8 (5)	5.0 (3)
Japan	5.4 (12)	8.9 (7=)	3.2 (1)	1.9 (1)	6.1 (7)
EC	3.5	9.3	8.4	6.9	6.8
OECD	2.9	8.3	6.9	5.1	5.9

B. By administrations

	1960-64	1965-70	1971-74	1975-79	1980-86
UK	2.9 (5=)	4.6 (8)	10.4 (10)	15.6 (12)	8.1 (9)
USA	1.2 (1)	3.8 (6)	6.2 (2)	8.1 (6)	6.1 (5=)
Japan	5.5 (12)	5.7 (11)	11.4 (11=)	7.3 (4)	3.2 (1)
EC	3.1	4.0	8.6	10.7	8.4
OECD	2.2	4.0	7.8	9.3	6.9

C. Before and after EC membership

	1960-72	1973-86	1973-86 (UK outside EC)
UK	4.5	11.3	10.5
EC	4.0	9.6	9.3
UK as % of EC	113.0%	119.0%	113.0%

Source: OECD 1986, IMF, national data. 12 countries are Belgium, Canada, Denmark, France, Germany, Ireland, Italy, Japan, Netherlands, Switzerland, UK, USA.

Lloyds Bank Economic Bulletin, Number 100, April, 1987.

MULTIPLE-CHOICE QUESTIONS

Page

A.   **THE USE OF MULTIPLE-CHOICE QUESTIONS** 122

B.   **TYPES OF MULTIPLE-CHOICE QUESTIONS** 123
   Simple-Completion Questions 123
   The Multiple-Completion Question 123
   Assertion-Reason Questions 124
   Matching Pairs Questions 127

C.   **CHECKLIST** 128

A. THE USE OF MULTIPLE-CHOICE QUESTIONS

The use of multiple-choice questions in examinations allows students to be examined in all aspects of the syllabus. This in turn means that it is necessary for you to understand all aspects of your work and makes it doubly important for you to find answers to anything you do not quite understand.

Throughout your course, the use of multiple-choice questions will act as an indicator of whether you have understood a section of the course or a particular topic. You have the opportunity to test yourself as well since there are increasing numbers of books now available which contain many multiple-choice questions on various topics. Take notice particularly of the books which not only give you the answer but also an explanation of why that particular answer is the correct one.

Multiple-choice questions can also provide an excellent revision aid. They can highlight weaknesses in your knowledge which you are then able to correct.

HINTS

Here are some general guidelines which you should follow when attempting multiple-choice questions. More specific guidelines are included in the next section.

(a) Read the question very carefully. It will have been written in a precise way, so check carefully just what is required in the answer.

(b) Have some idea of what the answer should be before looking at the list of possibilities. Some of the answers are put there deliberately to distract you, so do not let yourself be tempted into a wrong answer.

(c) Do not treat the questions as a lottery. Never just guess at an answer. There will always be some possibilities which you should be able to eliminate. Even if you are unsure of the answer, you should be able to narrow the possibilities down to just a couple.

(d) Always check your answers.

(e) If, when using questions as an aid to learning or for revision purposes, you answer incorrectly, be sure that you understand what the right answer is and why you got it wrong.

B. TYPES OF MULTIPLE-CHOICE QUESTIONS

The term multiple-choice question really refers to a number of different types of questions. There are actually four main types of question which are used in examinations:

Simple-Completion Questions

Simple-completion questions (called multiple-choice questions by some boards) require you to select one answer from four or five alternatives. Each question will require you to give a single unequivocal answer to a direct question or the correct completion of a statement.

EXAMPLES

1. A consumer who is maximising his/her utility will] stem

   A. equate the price of a good to its marginal utility

   B. buy cheap goods rather than expensive goods

   C. buy a good until its marginal utility is zero   distractors

   D. buy goods which have a utility greater than their price

   E. allocate his/her money between goods so that the price to marginal utility ratio is equal in all goods] key

2. The law of diminishing returns relates to the] stem

   A. marginal output of a fixed factor] distractor

   B. marginal output of a variable factor] key

   C. returns to scale

   D. average output of a variable factor   distractors

   E. total output

Notice that the question is referred to as the stem and the right answer as the key. Wrong answers are called distractors and that is exactly what they are. You must concentrate on the question to make sure you do not fall into any deliberate traps.

Read the stem slowly and beware especially of stems containing the word 'not'. Many students give wrong answers through reading the question too quickly, rather than through a lack of understanding.

The Multiple-Completion Question

The multiple-completion question may not necessarily have a single correct answer. A set of responses is provided and any or all of them may be relevant.

In this type of question there is a stem followed by four or five options, any of which may be correct. A response code is provided, which comprises alternative combinations of options. One of these options will be correct.

$\boxed{\text{EXAMPLES}}$

1. If a car manufacturer raised its price by 5% and, as a result, the volume of car sales fell by 3%, which of the following would be less than unity? — stem

    (i) the income elasticity of demand

    (ii) the cross-elasticity of demand

    — distractors

    (iii) the price elasticity of demand — correct option

    Choose A if only (i), (ii) and (iii) are correct
             B if only (i) and (ii) are correct
             C if only (ii) and (iii) are correct — response code
             D if only (i) is correct
             E if only (iii) is correct

2. Which of the following could result from a devaluation of the foreign exchange rate of sterling? — stem

    (i) a correction in the fundamental disequilibrium of the balance of payments — correct option

    (ii) a reduction in the cost of living

    (iii) an improvement in the terms of trade

    — distractors

    (iv) a fall in the exchange value of sterling balances held externally. — correct option

    Choose A if (i), (ii) and (iii) only are correct
             B if (i) and (iv) only are correct
             C if (ii) and (iv) only are correct — response code
             D if (iv) only is correct
             E if (i) and (iii) only are correct

Assertion-Reason Questions

This type of question comprises two statements. Each statement is either true or false, linked by the word 'because'. The first statement makes an assertion, that is to say, a positive statement or claim. The second statement purports to provide a valid or true reason for the first. If both the assertion and the reason are correct you must then decide whether or not the reason is a correct explanation of the assertion.

Thus there are five outcome combinations possible (see examples following table).

	Assertion	Reason	Argument
A.	True	True	Reason is a correct explanation of assertion
B.	True	True	Reason is not a correct explanation of assertion
C.	True	False	Not applicable
D.	False	True	Not applicable
E.	False	False	Not applicable

There is a logical way in which you ought to tackle a question like this, which can be seen from the flow chart below.

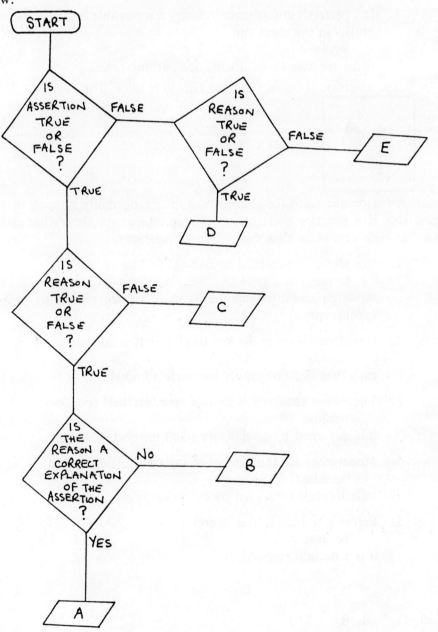

EXAMPLES

1. The Economic Problem can be characterised by lack of money
        because
    money can buy anything.

Clearly both the assertion and the reason are false, so, if we look back to our response table, we can see that the answer must be E.

2. Price elasticity varies along the length of a linear demand curve
        because
    at the top of the curve a proportionately small change in price yields a proportionately large change in quantity demanded, whereas at the bottom of the curve the opposite is the case.

Both the assertion and the reason are correct and the reason explains the assertion. Thus the key is A.

3. In a perfectly competitive industry it is possible for firms to earn super-normal profits in the short run
        because
    firms are able to sell their goods at any price.

The assertion is correct but the reason is false. The key is C.

EXERCISE

Below are five assertion-reason questions for you to attempt. Because this is a practice exercise, there is one answer for each key. Note that this would not normally happen in an examination. The questions are also rather easier than most A level questions.

1. Economics is regarded as a social science
        because
    although scientific method is used we are unable to perform laboratory experiments.

2. Interdependence is the key to oligopoly behaviour
        because
    each firm in an oligopoly has perfect knowledge of the reactions of its rivals.

3. The Soviet economy is known as a 'market' economy
        because
    it is governed by a relatively small number of people.

4. Monetarists see the control of inflation as important
        because
    inflation can be caused by excess aggregate demand.

5. Petrol is termed a 'free' good
        because
    it is a natural resource.

ANSWERS

1. A   2. C   3. D   4. B   5. E

Matching Pairs Questions

Matching pairs questions occur where there is a set of answers common to two or more questions. Each answer may be used once, more than once, or not at all. For example, you may be given a diagram or a set of data and asked two or three separate questions about it. The same options, A to E, are used for each question, and you must match each question to the correct option.

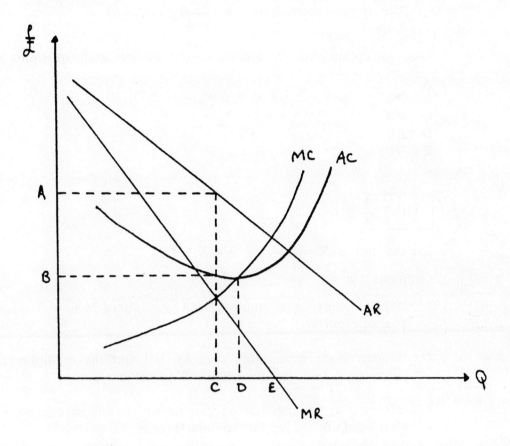

EXAMPLE 1

The diagram above shows cost and revenue curves for a monopolist. From the labels A to E select the appropriate price or output level indicated below:

1. The profit-maximising level of output.

2. The point at which additional sales result in a reduction of revenue.

3. The profit-maximising price.

⎤
⎥
⎥ Stem
⎥
⎦

     A. Key to 3
     B. Distractor
     C. Key to 1
     D. Distractor
     E. Key to 2

⎤
⎥
⎥ Options
⎥
⎦

EXAMPLE 2

The data below refers to an open economy with government activity.

Consumption	=	4000
Investment	=	1500
Government expenditure	=	2100
Imports	=	900

From the options A to E select the correct answers to the questions below:

A   0
B   200
C   400
D   900
E   7600

HINT

Use the formula $Y = C + I + G + X - M$.

Questions

1. If the economy is in equilibrium with an output of 7600, what is the level of exports?

2. If government expenditure rises by 100 and the multiplier is estimated to be 4, by how much will output increase?

3. If the country becomes a closed economy with no imports or exports, what would be the level of national income?

Stem

A.	Distractor
B.	Distractor
C.	Key to 2
D.	Key to 1
E.	Key to 3

Options

C.   **CHECKLIST**   √   √   √   √   √   √   √   √   √   √   √

1	Multiple-choice questions allow the examination of the whole syllabus.
2	Multiple-choice questions provide useful revision aids.
3	Do not guess when answering questions.
4	There are four main types of multiple-choice question.
5	Have an idea of the answer to a question before looking at the possibilities. Do not let 'distractors' distract.

PROJECTS

Page

A. **INTRODUCTION** 130

B. **THE TOPIC** 130
    Pitfalls 130
    The Final Title 132

C. **PLANNING YOUR PROJECT** 133
    Preliminary Reading 133
    The Outline Plan 133
    Further Information 133

D. **COLLECTING, SELECTING AND ORGANISING INFORMATION** 135

E. **THE STRUCTURE OF THE PROJECT** 137
    The Title Page 137
    The Abstract 137
    Acknowledgements 137
    Contents 137
    Introduction 138
    The Body of the Project Divided into Chapters 138
    Conclusions 138
    Appendices 138
    References 138
    Bibliography 138

F. **WRITING UP THE PROJECT** 139
    Style 139
    Quotations 139
    Illustrative Material 139

G. **CHECKLIST** 140

A. INTRODUCTION

There are many different types of project and many names for the finished product: dissertation, thesis, fieldwork, report, extended essay, etc. Not all projects are the same, but this chapter attempts to bring together advice in order to help you produce as good a project as you can.

The purposes of project work are listed below:
- To encourage some independent thought
- To develop an ability to find, interpret and present material
- To find out whether students are capable of putting into practice some of the theories and principles learned in the course
- To give the student experience of organising material on a large scale
- To broaden the student's knowledge and understanding of a particular topic

A project may be the longest piece of writing you are asked to do. This might seem like an awesome task at the outset, but it can be very satisfying for a number of reasons:

(a) If you are interested in the topic, you can spend time on your project, thus providing a continuous source of pleasure.

(b) It is satisfying to be able to study a topic in more depth than would usually be the case with essay-writing.

(c) At the end of the exercise you will have produced a very satisfying result.

(d) A successful project testifies that you are capable of hard work and will make a good impression with potential employers.

(e) Your work may form the basis for further research in future.

It should now be obvious that one of the most important decisions you have to make is the choice of your topic.

B. THE TOPIC

From the very outset, it is important that you make contact with the person who is to supervise your project. This may be one of your teachers or somebody else. Your project tutor will be able to advise you on the practicalities of your choice. For example, if there is very limited information on a topic, it may be better to choose something else.

On the other hand, you must choose a topic in which you are genuinely interested. If you find a topic boring, then the project will become a dull exercise. Good projects rarely come from students who dislike the topic they have studied.

Pitfalls

When choosing your topic, there are some points worth bearing in mind. The following pitfalls can and should be avoided:

(a) Do not choose a topic which is too large. It is often easy to underestimate the size of a topic.

(b) Do not choose a topic which is too complex for the level at which you are studying.

(c) Choose a topic for which material is readily available. If you are working to a tight time schedule, you do not want to spend the bulk of this searching for information.

(d) Do not choose a topic where information may be confidential. This is particularly important to bear in mind if you are interested in looking at a particular firm. The firm may be unlikely to let you have certain items of information.

In all these cases, *consult your tutor.*

> EXAMPLES

Title: The Tourist Industry in the U.K.

Comment: This sounds like an interesting title and there is certainly a lot of information about it. But you will probably find that there is in fact too much. The project seems too big from the outset. It may have been chosen by somebody who already has contacts in this area. A good idea might therefore be to narrow it down to, for example, Tourism in South Hampshire, or Holidays for the Over Sixties. In this way there is something more specific to look at. In both instances there will be people and organisations who will be able to provide a lot of information.

Title: An Analysis of the Growth of the U.K. Computer Market

Comment: This sounds like another interesting project. A lot of consideration would have to go into where the information was to come from. Perhaps a couple of computer manufacturers could be used as case studies—if they were willing. There should be some statistics relating to this area, but they might be rather complicated. Again, it might be worth trying to narrow the field a little.

Title: The Decline of the Coal Industry in South Wales

Comment: There has been a lot written on this topic, and so, when collecting material, you would have to be very selective. This would be very time-consuming. There are many people in the area who could be contacted—trade unions, British Coal and perhaps retired miners. It might not be a feasible project unless you lived in South Wales, however. There ought to be lots of statistics available locally. A case study of the impact on a local mining village might be a good idea—indeed this would probably be enough to constitute a good project on its own.

EXERCISE

The following is a list of project titles. Comment on whether or not you consider each project to be a viable one. State your reasons:

Inflation in the 1970s and 1980s.

The Costs and Benefits of the Channel Tunnel.

The Wages of Women Employees in Local Firms.

Trade between Japan and England in the Nineteenth Century.

The Demand for Houses in the Local Area.

The Economics of Acid Rain.

Third World Debt.

Advertising in National Newspapers.

Regional Policy in the 1980s.

The Final Title

Although from the outset you will know what you are studying and will have followed an outline plan (explained in the next section), as you proceed you may find that the project takes a slightly different course to that anticipated. This is often the case with project work. Once the project is nearing its end you should review the title to see that it still adequately reflects the content of your work. Be prepared to change it therefore.

The final project title should satisfy the following criteria:

- It should convey an accurate picture of what the project is about.
- It should sound interesting to the reader.
- It should not mislead the reader. If the reader expects something which is not in the project, this may prove disappointing. If it conveys the wrong idea to the marker, it may cost you marks.
- It should not be too long. If you consider that the contents of the project cannot be reflected in a short phrase, consider using a title with subtitle.

C. PLANNING YOUR PROJECT

Preliminary Reading

Preliminary reading is vital for two reasons:
- To find out how much material is available
- To learn more about the subject and reduce the subject to manageable proportions

Your starting point will be to look at general references such as text books, encyclopaedias and dictionaries. Simply browsing through these should give you some idea of the various aspects of your topic. This will enable you to pin-point a particular line along which to proceed.

☐ Do not spend too long doing this. A more detailed search for information will come later.

☐ Note possible sources of information.

☐ If you find a useful article, then also note some of the references which were used in writing it. These may be useful to you as well.

☐ Consult your teacher and the librarian. They may come up with more ideas as you proceed.

The Outline Plan

Your next step will be to draw up an outline plan. This should indicate the approach to be adopted and include a list of references already consulted and a list of those you plan to look at. This outline will form a good basis for discussion with your tutor.

It will be useful if you can plan the contents of your project alongside sources of information, or ideas about where you may get the information. A useful way of doing this is to divide your page into two parallel halves.

EXAMPLE

Let us suppose that you have decided that an interesting study would be an examination of the impact on trades unions of the introduction of information technology. On the next page is an outline plan of the way you might proceed.

What to note from the plan:
1. There is plenty of room for additions.
2. The content is broken down into four main sections with sub-sections. This follows a logical progression.

3. The right-hand side contains notes of preliminary reading, ideas of things to do (usually followed by question marks) and action to be taken (e.g. write letters).
4. The plan should not be seen as rigid. For example, if local firms are not willing to discuss the introduction of I.T. with you, then something else can take the place of that idea.
5. At the present time no indication of the length of each section is given. This should be possible at a later stage, as you manage to select and organise your information.

EXERCISE

Draw up an outline plan for one of the following project titles:

    The Common Agricultural Policy.
    Local House Prices in the Past Twelve
        Months.
    North Sea Oil Production.

Further Information

You should be familiar with the use of a library before you start your project, and the library catalogue should be one of your first points of reference. Your research will often involve you in searching through many books and documents. There are a number of reference works which can help make this search a lot easier. The librarian can help you with this, but important sources to note include:

> *The British Education Index;*
> *Contents of Recent Economics Journals*
>   *(COREJ);*
> *Social Science Citation Index.*

Books and papers not in the library can usually be obtained on request via your local library from the National Lending Library service. Librarians are often very keen to help and will happily discuss your work with you.

It will often be the case that you will wish to write to certain people and organisations about your work. Keep a copy of the letters you send. Even if you do not receive a reply, these letters provide evidence of research activity. You should be awarded some marks for this, even if it proves to be unsuccessful.

Trade Unions and the Introduction of Information Technology

CONTENT	SOURCES/ACTION
Impact on Employment – employment loss – employment creation – evidence	include economic theory – replacement of labour with capital. (See Smith ch. 7) find some statistics ?? ask librarian
Response of T.U. movement – policies – attitudes	look in Industrial Relations Journal. Policy documents Question T.U. leaders? } letters*
Case Studies	News International Case Study? Local firms ??? (letters?)
The Future – role of labour as a factor of production – role of trade unions – the workerless factory? – role of leisure?	See 'Economist' article 12.7.87 questionnaire? } find out about T.U.* reactions to part-time work and job sharing <u>Also:</u> Griffiths + Wall Ch. 10 for overview

D. COLLECTING, SELECTING AND ORGANISING INFORMATION

Before reading this section, it may be useful for you to go back and have another look at the chapter on making notes.

The collection and subsequent selection and organisation of information will be a very important part of your project. Only if this is done well will you subsequently be able to write up a good project. Material will be collected throughout the period of the project. This will mean you should have many notes, some of which you should be prepared to discard—but not throw away, as they may be useful at a later date. Always bear the following approaches in mind:

(a) Even in the early stages of preliminary reading, searching and collecting material, be active and critical. Ask yourself how useful certain pieces of information might be. Do not waste time looking at peripheral information, but note its source just in case you decide to return to it.

(b) Do not be afraid to change and adapt your project plan in the early stages of information collection as you find what is and what is not available.

(c) Be active and critical when you select the material you are going to use. The quality of your final project will be determined partly by the information which goes into it. Do not use information which is inappropriate just because it fills a space.

(d) Before you write each section of your project, make sure the information which you are going to use has been organised into a logical and sensible order. Have everything you need before you start. There is nothing worse than getting half-way through a chapter and finding that you do not have one of your sources. Spending time finding it can interrupt your concentration and make your work disjointed.

EXERCISE

Do some preliminary reading for one of the projects for which you drew up an outline plan. To what extent are you forced to adapt that plan in the light of availability of information?

EXAMPLE

One way of dealing with the mass of information which you will have to organise is to use record cards. These are compact and easy to arrange in a logical order. They should contain pieces of information, sources of other useful material, comments about the usefulness of that material, ideas for further development of the project and comments about where the material might fit into the final project.

On page 136 is an example of how record cards can be used to organise information. These are the first three cards for a project on multinational enterprises in the U.K. Note that they contain brief information, references to additional information, and ideas for further research. Together they form what could be an introduction to the project.

MULTINATIONAL ENTERPRISES IN THE U.K.　1

Introduction:
　　See Griffiths & Wall Ch. 7

Definition:
　　'an enterprise which owns production facilities
　　outside the country in which it is based'

　　But n.b. other definitions

　　n.b. difference between multinational
　　　　and transnational company.

　　　　　　　　　　　　　　　　　　　　2

Largest multinationals/transnationals in the
world : Exxon, General Motors, Ford (U.S.A)
　　　　　Royal Dutch Shell, Philips, B.A.T,
　　　　　Volkswagen, B.P, Unilever (Europe)

The output of these companies is growing
at 10-15% per annum. (See Dunning Book).

n.b. Find out about Japanese multinationals.

　　　　　　　　　　　　　　　　　　　　3

THE BIG FOUR: (U.K)

Unilever (Food) Sales (1982) £24 bn. (48% foreign)
　　　　44% foreign employment
ICI (Chemicals) Sales (1982) £13 bn. (61% foreign)
　　　　35% for. emp.
GEC (Electronics) Sales (1983) £7bn. (50% foreign)
GKN (Engineering) Sales (1982) £5 bn. (42% ")
　　　　[See U.N. Yearbook]

　　　　　　　　　　　　　　　　　　　　etc.

E. THE STRUCTURE OF THE PROJECT

Although you should write the main body of your project first, you should be aware of the overall structure of the project from the outset. The following structure should normally be adopted:

The Title Page

Include the following in your title page:
—The title of the project
—The name of the author
—The name of the institution
—The date of completion of the project
The title itself may be slightly different from the one specified at the outset. It should usually be short and yet indicate the content of the project as accurately as possible.

The Abstract

This is a summary of the report and should be about 100–200 words in length. It should give the reader a framework, demonstrating the main features of the project and any conclusions reached.

> EXAMPLE

There follows an example of an abstract. It is taken from the beginning of a project which examines the economic and some psychological consequences of redundancy.

This study is an examination of the economic and psychological effects of redundancy. A sample of adults who were made unemployed were interviewed. Their attitudes towards their families and towards society in general were examined. A group of adults who were not made redundant were also studied. They acted as a control group. In each case, the unemployed group admitted personal distress and said their family relationships had deteriorated. These findings are discussed in terms of the wider economic and social costs often associated with unemployment.

Acknowledgements

This section should be used to record thanks to people and institutions who have been particularly helpful in the compilation of the report.

Contents

The table of contents should provide the reader with a detailed structure for the report by giving headings and associated page numbers.

Thus the title, abstract and contents provide the reader with information from which he or she can determine whether the report is relevant to him/her.

Introduction

The introduction should provide background information about the project area. This could consist of the sequence of events leading up to one particular event, or the results of earlier investigations. Normally the introduction to the project will be between 300 and 500 words. The introduction should also be used:
—to state the aims of the project;
—to discuss the approach which has been used in the research;
—to state any assumptions upon which the work is based;
—to interest people in reading the rest of the work.

The Body of the Project Divided into Chapters

This should contain the information found during research and preparation. It should be presented logically and lead on towards the conclusion. Headings and sub-headings should be used to act as clear indicators of what is being discussed. Accurate English and a readable style are important. These are discussed in section F.

Conclusions

The conclusion will not normally contain new information. It will summarise the discussion in the main body of the project and evaluate any results achieved. The conclusion should make points which link together the various aspects of your work and make suggestions about how it might be extended. The conclusion may also make recommendations or comments following naturally from the main discussion.

Appendices

An appendix should be used for information which is relevant to the discussion in the main body of the project, but which, if presented there, would distract the reader from the main argument. This will often be the case with lengthy tables of statistics or computer print-outs.

References

There are a number of ways in which references can be cited. You must check to see whether there is a particular way in which your references have to be presented.

One very common way of presenting the references is as follows. Slightly different styles are used depending on the source of the reference.

1. For an article in a periodical or journal:

Borrie, G., 'Competition, Mergers and Price-fixing', *Lloyds Bank Review*, 1987, Number 164, pp. 1–15

2. For an article, paper or chapter in a book:

Kregel, J. A., 'Income Distribution', in: Eichner, (ed.), *A Guide to Post-Keynesian Economics* (Macmillan, London, 1979), pp. 46–60

3. For a book:

Glahe, F. R., *Macroeconomics: Theory and Policy* (Harcourt Brace Jovanovich, New York, 1977)

Bibliography

This is a further list of references not directly mentioned in the text but which have been extensively used in the preparation of the project. These can be regarded as useful additional reading, and you may, if you wish, add comments to each entry.

F. WRITING UP THE PROJECT

By the time you come to start the process of writing up your project, you should have rejected unwanted material and organised your notes in a structured way according to a plan. (You may like to look back at the section on constructing plans in the chapter on essay-writing.)

Make sure that you have a large supply of paper and be careful not to overcrowd a page, allowing space for corrections.

As you write, you should work through your notes, putting them aside as you progress. You will often find that linking themes and important points come to mind as you write. Keep a piece of paper at hand ready to note these down for inclusion later in the project, or in the conclusion.

It is useful if you divide the writing process into manageable tasks, setting yourself deadlines by which each part should be completed.

Style
☐ The project must be well written, containing no errors of spelling or punctuation.
☐ The style should be clear and concise.
☐ A formal style of writing should be employed. This means that abbreviations and colloquialisms should not be used.
☐ The use of 'I' should be avoided wherever possible, so as to give the impression of impartiality.
☐ Imagine that you are writing for an intelligent but uninformed reader.

Quotations

Quotations can add interest to the text and show that you have researched the topic. In general, though, too much quoting can be a bad thing. The best quotation is a short one. Quotations should be completely accurate.

Short quotations can be placed within the body of the text surrounded by quotation marks. It is normal for longer quotations (more than two sentences) to be placed between paragraphs and indented, so that they stand out. The source of the quotation should be included and a full reference given at the end of the project.

Illustrative Material

Tables, graphs, diagrams, drawings, maps and photographs should only be included if they convey a piece of information more clearly than the written word. Far from improving a project, irrelevant information can detract from it.

Illustrative material should be as clear as possible. Too much detail will make it difficult to understand. All illustrations must be given a number and a title.

G.   CHECKLIST   √   √   √   √   √   √   √   √   √   √   √

1	Choose your topic carefully. Make sure it is something in which you are interested.
2	Do not choose a topic which is too broad or too complex.
3	Consult with your tutor regularly. She/he will be a very valuable source of help and advice.
4	Time spent on preliminary general reading will be time well spent.
5	Make use of the library and the librarian.
6	Select and organise your material carefully. Make sure that it follows a logical order.
7	Your project should follow the structure laid out in section D.
8	When writing up your project, pay particular attention to style.
9	A full set of references should appear in a consistent format at the end of the project.

REVISION

		Page
A.	**PLANNING YOUR REVISION**	142
	Drawing up a Plan	142
	Using Time Effectively	142
	Working Independently	142
	Timing and Strategy	142
B.	**REVISION ACTIVITIES**	145
	The Process of Revision	145
	1. Revising	145
	2. Reviewing	145
	3. Remembering	145
C.	**REVIEW, RECALL AND REVISION NOTES**	149
	Revision Cards	149
	Revision Notes from Revision Notes	150
	Cluster Revision	150
	Diagrams and Revision Notes	152
	Rapid Review and Recall	152
D.	**REMEMBERING INFORMATION**	152
E.	**ADDITIONAL POINTS TO REMEMBER**	154
F.	**CHECKLIST**	156

A. PLANNING YOUR REVISION

To some extent you will be revising work through-out your period of study. We have already men-tioned the fact that once you have made notes, they ought to be updated, amended and reviewed periodically and it was suggested that you stick to some kind of schedule. In your final revision period before the examination, these points become even more important.

When to start final revision is a difficult deci-sion to make and will depend partly on the demands which your other courses of study make on you. However, it is good to start with some review of all subject matter in the term before the Easter prior to the examination. It will be impor-tant to revise all your subjects fully, so a 'plan of campaign' will be essential.

Drawing up a Plan

When deciding on your revision plan, you must make sure that you are doing enough work, whilst allowing yourself time for other activities. Too much work can make you overtired and then time spent on revision will be wasted. Be realistic. It is so easy to start by being over-ambitious in setting tasks and this can lead to your abandonment of the programme. It is also very easy to start with good intentions but later let your work slide. If you are purposeful and organised, this is less likely to happen.

A typical work schedule for a week appears on page 143. Notice that one day is left completely free from work as long as the tasks earlier in the week have been completed. This acts as an incen-tive to follow the schedule. On the other hand, do not stick so rigidly to your plan as to exclude the possiblity of doing some other subject revision if something crops up to stimulate that. The second work schedule shows how you might modify your plan both to take in an unexpected night out and in order to follow a particular urge to revise History rather than Geography. Modifying your plan does not mean just leaving things out, however.

You will also find it useful to sketch out a more long-term plan covering the topics you intend to revise week by week. Do not revise new topics right up to the examination. This will only mean that

you will forget the ones you revised in previous weeks. The final couple of weeks before the exam should be used for consolidation and committing information to memory.

Using Time Effectively

At School/College
It is all too easy not to revise during a free period or to seem to revise but actually achieve very little. It is important not to allow yourself to be distracted. Many short revision blocks are usually more effective than long-drawn-out periods, which often turn into hours of staring at pages of work without taking much in. At school therefore, do not use the excuse that, as you only have thirty minutes (or less) available, it is not worth doing anything.

At Home
If you are revising in the evening, give yourself short breaks between tasks. Short revision spells of between fifteen and thirty minutes should be broken up with five-minute breaks. Discipline yourself to stick to five minutes and in that time just rest your eyes, hands and brain, and perhaps walk around a little or make a cup of coffee.

Working Independently

You will realise that working towards an A level involves much independent study. This is even more true when it comes to final revision periods. Because you have great freedom in organising your time, self-discipline is needed to get the most from that time. Keep in mind that a successful end result will be worth the hard work, but that success at A level will only be achieved if that hard work is done.

Timing and Strategy

After a period of time, you should realise how best you yourself revise. Mock examinations can often give you the opportunity of working out your revi-sion timing in preparation for the final examina-tion period. Precise timing and technique will be up to you. Discuss strategies with others, but try to work out what is best for you. The rest of this chapter looks at the strategies which you could try out and use.

1.

	MON	TUES	WED	THURS	FRI
FREE PERIODS/ PRIVATE STUDY	Economics (30 min)	History (30 min) Geog (30 min)	Economics (30 min) Geog (30 min)	History (30 min) Geog (1hr)	Econ. (1hr)
EVENING	History 1hr Geog 1hr	Economics 1hr History 1hr	Geog 1hr	Economics 1hr History 2hrs	

	SAT	SUN
MORNING		Econ. 2 hrs Hist 1hr
AFTERNOON		Geog 2 hrs

2.

	MON	TUES	WED	THURS	FRI
FREE PERIODS/ PRIVATE STUDY	Economics (30 min)	History (30 min) Geog (30 min)	Economics (30 min) Geog (30 min)	History (30 min) Geog (1hr)	Econ. (1hr)
EVENING	History 1hr Geog 1hr	Economics 1hr History 1hr	Geog 1hr	Economics 1hr History 2hrs	

	SAT	SUN
MORNING	Econ 1hr Hist 1½ hrs	Econ. 2 hrs Hist 1hr
AFTERNOON		Geog 1½ hrs Hist 2 hrs

REVISION PLAN   (ECONOMICS)

WEEK	TOPICS	ADDITIONS | CHANGES
1	Methodology The Economic Problem	
2	Economic Systems Supply and Demand	
3	Theory of Costs / Theory of the Firm Nationalisation / Privatisation	
4	Microeconomic Policy and Regional Policy Distribution: Wages, Rent etc.	
5	Finance and Public Finance	
6	National Income Accounting Unemployment	
7	Classical Theory of U. Keynesian Economics Multiplier etc.	
8	Monetarism Government Macro Policies	
9	Exchange rates The Open Economy	
10	International Trade	
11	Unemployment and Inflation Contemporary Topics in Economics	
12		
13	Final Revision	
14	Final Revision	
15	Final Revision	
16	Monday a.m Exam Thursday p.m Exam	

B. REVISION ACTIVITIES

Revision is an active process which covers a number of different skills and activities which together constitute effective revision.

The Process of Revision

By the time you reach your examination, you should have sufficient detail and range of knowledge to be able to tackle all the compulsory questions and, where you have a choice, to be able to select the questions in which you can perform most effectively. It is important that you understand all your work as you go along, since, when it comes to final revision, it will be time wasted if you are having to learn new concepts.

Poor revision techniques, such as learning by rote for hours, can in fact hinder rather than help matters. If you revise in a superficial way or only to a limited extent, you will not have the knowledge or skills required to answer A level questions.

We can divide the process of revision into three parts:

1. *Revising:* The amending, editing, re-working and addition of notes.
2. *Reviewing:* The re-reading of notes for recall and the establishment of logical order.
3. *Remembering:* The recall and memorising of information.

Revision is a continuous process. It should start as soon as you put pen to paper in your first Economics lesson and will be a progressive task becoming more and more important the nearer you get to the examination. Let us consider the three elements of revision as stages to be followed during your period of study.

STAGE 1: REVISING

Your ability to take notes will improve as you progress through your course, but they will always need revising in some way. In the main, you should be attempting to add notes and rework notes as you go on and as you come across additional information. Thus this first stage should begin very early on in your course. The more you are able to revise your notes and correct any weaknesses throughout the course, the more time you will be able to devote to the other two stages in your final revision period.

EXAMPLE

Look at the notes which appear on page 146. These are an example of some early notes taken in a lesson, which now need revising. The second set of notes (p.147) contains some additional material which the student has taken from a book. In the margins of both sets of notes are comments and questions.

Consider the following points as well:

(a) In the early notes there are definitions of the sectors of the economy, which are very well known to the student now because they have been used so much in subsequent work.

(b) The notes from the book contain a lot of statistics which will never be remembered as they are. Some sort of rationalisation process is required.

Think about how you would revise these notes, then turn to page 148 to see how they have been changed.

Do you think the process has been carried out well?

What else could have been added to the notes?

How might the notes be useful at a later stage?

STAGE 2: REVIEWING

Once you have revised your notes, you are in a position to review them. Essentially your task is to re-read your notes critically and carefully in order to strengthen your understanding and recognise links, interrelationships and logical progressions to and from other parts of your work.

Reviewing your notes is closely tied up with recall. The more carefully you read your notes, the better will be your eventual powers of recall. The important thing is that you should be thinking about the information contained in your notes.

STAGE 3: REMEMBERING

Regular reviewing will help your recall of information. The fact is that, like it or not, you must be able to memorise a certain amount of information to take into the exam with you. It is important to remember, however, that re-reading material will not on its own be the most effective way of remembering things. The emphasis must be on active methods of revision.

Structure of the U.K. Economy

Like all economys we can divide it into 3
sectors:
    1. Primary (Agriculture, Mining, Farming...)
    2. Secondary / Manufacturing
              (car manufacture, consumer durables:
              anything made from raw materials)
    3. Tertiary / Service (insurance, banking
                      etc. etc.)

Primary sector is the smallest sector in proportion to
the others. Secondary sector is declining and service
sector growing rapidly. One reason for this
is rising personal incomes of those in work, this
leads to demand for things like leisure and
financial protection of family => life assurance.

Second. production is a feature of the modern economy.
In 1980 35% of the population were employed in
this sector.

Tertiary production includes transportation, retailing,
govt. services (e.g. education). All commercial services.

% employed in Tertiary Sector

UK: 1901 40%   1980: Portugal 33%
       1950 46%   Greece 28%
       1970 51%   U.S.A 62%
       1980 60%

The balance between the 3 sectors gives an
indication of the state of development of the
economy. A high prop'n in Tertiary -> Advanced.
But in advanced econ. there are dangers of not
having enough people manufacturing goods.
Less developed economies have a high prop.n of
people working in Primary Sector.

economies

Tertiary sector
provides many
exports
(invisibles)
<u>see</u> later

Statistics
for Third
World ?

What
dangers ?

U.K. Economic Structure   (Griffiths & Wall Ch.1)

Primary Sector   (1980 = 100)

	1973	1984
Agric. forestry & fishing	87.4	119
Coal and coke	114	33.8
Extraction of oil and gas	2.2	147.1

Secondary Sector

Mineral oil processing	126.9	98.4
Manufacturing	114.1	100
Construction	122.4	98.6

Manufacturing actually fell 15.5 points between 1979 and 1981 although it recovered between 1981 and 1984. Even so, U.K. manuf. o/p in 1984 was below its 1969 level.

This record of decline in the production industries has not been experienced by other industrial market economies. Their production increased at an average of 6.2% per year between 1960 and 1970, slowing down to 2.3% per year between 1970 and 1983 (still higher than the U.K)

Industrial economies = developed countries.

In the tertiary sector output grew in every sub-sector between 1964 and 1979. But since 1979 output has fallen in two of the sectors (Distribution/hotels/catering and transport). Even the service sector growth has been below that of other industrial economies.

REVISION NOTES
Structure of the U.K. Economy

Primary Sector

Smallest sector. (In less developed countries it is large relative to other sectors).
In UK there has been a significant decline in production/extraction of coal and coke but massive increase in extraction of oil and gas.

Secondary Sector – a feature of industrialised economies

Manuf. o/p fell between 1979 and 1981 although recovered slightly after 1981. In 1984, though, it was still below 1969 level. Manuf. o/p worse than in other indust. economies.

In 1980 33% of U.K. popn. employed in this sector.

Tertiary Sector

In 1980 60% of U.K. popn. in this sector.
The larger this sector, the more advanced the economy (e.g U.K. slightly smaller than U.S.A. but bigger than Portugal). Even in this sector the U.K. growth rate has been less than competitors'. Tertiary sector provides most of U.K. invisible exports.

Dangers

In advanced economies the danger is not having enough people producing manufactured goods. => Must import more (e.g cars)
   B of P defecit
   Wealth creation problems?

EXERCISE

One way of actively trying to recall information is to work on past questions from examination papers.

Look at two or three old examination questions, or some of the essay questions in Chapter 3. How far can you get with preparing essay plans? Try this at first untimed, and later within a strict time limit.

How much could you remember?

Keep returning to this sort of practice. It will be an active way of remembering things as well as pin-pointing weaknesses in your knowledge.

Review, recall and the making of revision notes are so interrelated that we will now devote a whole section to them.

C. REVIEW, RECALL AND REVISION NOTES

The review of work will greatly increase recall but weaknesses may still exist. Work needs to be done to rectify this by reworking material in an active way. It will be necessary for you to experiment with a few techniques of review and recall until you find one which suits your needs. Remember that information still makes up the bulk of your notes and the techniques discussed below will help your recall and understanding of this material.

Revision Cards

You may find it useful to make revision points on a set of cards. This was discussed briefly in the chapter on note-making, so look back at that if you think this might be useful. But try to make the system do more than just reproduce your notes. Ask yourself questions about linking themes, cross-references and interrelationships. As revision cards are easily carried it is a good idea to take the cards with you to look at when you have a free moment.

Revision Notes from Revision Notes

Your original notes are your first set of revision notes, but often these are lengthy and at times repetitive. As you review your notes, it is a good idea to make notes from your notes. At a later stage you may like to make notes from this new set, and so on. There are dangers in doing this, so follow the guidelines below:

(a) When you make notes from notes, you should not just copy word for word. Make extensive use of abbreviations and note what you consider to be most important or what you think you are likely to forget. Put the notes to one side and try to recall what you have written.

(b) If you keep making notes from notes, eventually you should end up with a list of important points which may lend themselves to a card index.

(c) Remember that, although useful, this can be a lengthy process.

(d) Once you have arrived at a final set of revision notes, do not use these alone for your final revision. Refer back to the original set of notes as well, to remind yourself of what goes between your main points. Remember that it was the process of making the notes from notes over and over again which was the useful activity.

Cluster Revision

The idea behind cluster revision is to use clusters of information based on a question and to formulate new questions based on the cluster and supporting points. The stages which are used in cluster revision are as follows:

(a) Decide on a topic, key points and supporting material. The topic should be decided upon by asking yourself a question, for example: *What was the cause of high inflation in the 1970s?*

(b) A number of key points are then thought of, each of which might represent a paragraph in the final essay.

(c) The question is placed on the horizontal axis and the key points on the vertical axis of the chart. See page 151.

(d) An associated question is posed, e.g. *What made oil an important factor in the problem?*

(e) A number of questions are posed and the chart is built up.

(f) In the intersecting boxes, comments are added to explain the significance or relationship of the key points to the question.

EXAMPLE

and

EXERCISE

In the example on page 151 the following questions were asked:

(i) *What was the cause of high inflation in the 1970s?*

(ii) *What made oil an important factor in the problem?*

(iii) *Why is high inflation such a problem?*

(iv) *What policies were used to try to rectify the situation?*

(v) *What impact did the problems of the 1970s have on the government's policies in the 1980s?*

Use this system to draw up a set of revision notes, beginning with the question: *Why is it sometimes asserted that government policy between 1979 and 1986 created over one million unemployed people?*

What are the benefits of cluster revision?

		High inflation of 1970's	Why is oil an important factor?	Why is inflation a problem?	Policies used to rectify the situation	Policies of 1980s (1979 – 198
1.	Expansion of money supply	Early 1970's				
	Oil	Exogenous shock	*		SAVE IT policies	
	Go for Growth Policies	Early 1970's			abandoned	growth declined in early 1980'
	No monetary control	Until 1976		Cuts might be made		rectified
2.	Oil rises four-fold		Not a small increase			
	Important energy source		Impact on Industry			
	U.K not a significant oil exporter then		B of P problems			
3.	Uncertainty			Partic. for I decisions	MTFS	MTFS
	Fixed incomes			Decline in real value		
	International competitiveness			B of P problems and low export revenue		
	Exchange rate problems		oil prices			
4.	Monetary control				1976	important
	Incomes Policies	Not very successful			Not totally successful	abandoned
	Price Controls				n.b. Bread	abandoned
5.	M.T.F.S				Planning	Centre stage
	Monetary targets	1976 IMF			*	for control but also confidence implications for u?
	Reduction in PSBR				*	
	Privatisation/ Deregulation.				*	Ideology: cost cutting

- Cluster revision involves all three revision activities—revising, reviewing and remembering. It can change the sequence of your notes and make you think of many more interrelationships which at first were not apparent. Cluster revision provides a new flexible structure to your notes.
- It is important that you learn to assess information for its worth and relevance. Cluster revision requires you to select information which is important and in context. This is a vital skill when answering an examination question.
- Cluster revision is a critical and active task, and, as such, will improve both your understanding and the quality of your revision notes.
- Cluster revision lends itself to the writing of essays.

Diagrams and Revision Notes

In many topics in Economics, the use of diagrams is very important. Revision notes should incorporate these diagrams where appropriate. In some topics, the use of a diagram can even help review and ultimately committal to memory.

EXAMPLE

Look at the set of diagrams on page 153, which illustrates the theory of perfect competition in both the short run and the long run. Since the theory is in fact just a logical progression of the diagrams, so long as you understand and can explain the diagrams and remember the key assumptions behind them, very little else is required.

Rapid Review and Recall

As the examination gets nearer, you might like to use this method of review which will also help you to memorise material. Carefully read a page from your file and turn the page. On rough paper jot down briefly all that you can remember.

Look back and see what you have missed. Without dwelling on the parts you could not recall, go on to the next page. Work through a

topic in this way and then go back and start again. When you repeat the process, your stock of knowledge of the topic should have increased and the amount you forget should eventually dwindle to nothing.

D. REMEMBERING INFORMATION

We have already discussed methods of revising and reviewing which will add to your ability to recall. Moreover, in the examination, the process of concentration will often allow you to recall information buried deep in your memory. However, to assume that the review of material is enough in itself to enable you to memorise it would be wrong.

In this section we look at methods of recall. Remember, though, that as with all revision tasks, memorising should be done purposefully and actively. Try a number of different revision methods to see which suits you best.

- *Recall by Points*
In any topic, seeing the subject matter as a number of points can significantly help you to memorise it. You might like to look back to Chapter 2, where note-making covers both the use of numbered points and the use of mnemonics to help you memorise.

- *Recall by Mental Picture*
If your revision notes are clear and concise, you can often form a mental picture of these in your mind. If you find it easy to make picture notes (see Chapter 2), for example, these can aid revision significantly.

- *Recall of Diagrams*
It is particularly important to remember that if you use diagrams in an examination they should be accurate. It is therefore imperative that you memorise these by drawing them out at random and checking to see if they are correct. It will be useful for you to have a checklist of all the diagrams you need to remember and to make sure you can draw each one on demand. Once you have memorised a diagram, you will often find that the associated theory and explanation come quite easily.

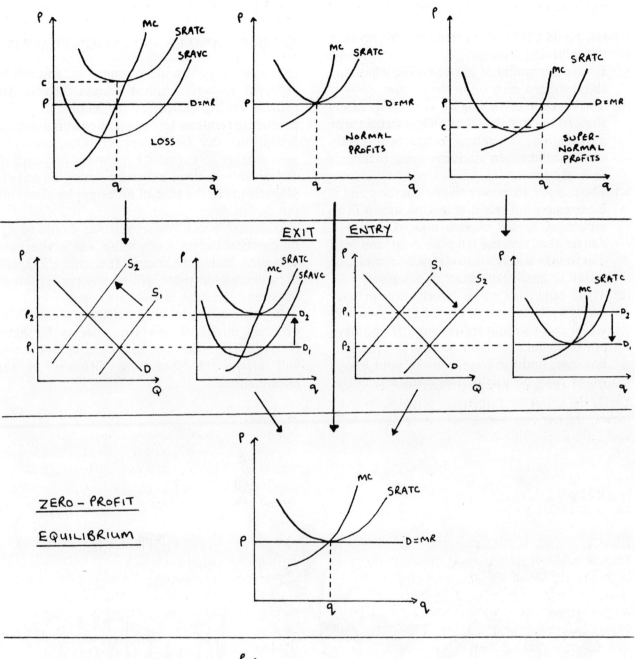

E. ADDITIONAL POINTS TO REMEMBER

USING ESSAYS FOR REVISION

Essays should not be used extensively for revision for the following reasons:

(a) Essays are bound to have failings, especially those written early on in the course.

(b) The purpose of writing an essay is to assess some of the skills of selection and structure of information. Therefore essays will rarely contain all the information relevant to a more general topic.

(c) The essay is an answer to *one* question and it is extremely unlikely that this question will be replicated in the examination. There is a danger that revising from an essay can lead you to take a very narrow view of a topic, or to fail to answer the exact question set.

(d) There ought not to be information in your essays which is not also in your files; these will be far more helpful for revision. If you have not kept your notes up-to-date in this fashion, however, and there are notes in your essays which may be useful, use them selectively, noting any comments made by your teacher on the essay.

REVISION AND EXAMINATION PRACTICE

In the period before the examination, you will be expected to write 'timed' essays, which will provide both practice for the examination and practice in recall under examination conditions. It is important that, besides answering questions that your teacher sets, you ask questions of yourself. Try to answer them either by timing an answer yourself or, in the case of an essay, by sketching out a plan.

Questions which you set yourself should be significantly different from those which you have answered during the course. It is unlikely that in the examination there will be any replication of questions you have already answered.

If you cannot think up sufficient numbers of different questions, ask your teacher for help. Never rewrite essays you have done before. There will always be something different in the examinations.

A good idea may be to work with friends in pairs, threes or in a syndicate. If each of you writes a different essay under examination conditions, it can be useful to look at each other's attempts, and make constructive comments. This in itself can help you remember points.

Alternatively, pairs, threes, or members of the syndicate could each plan an answer to the same examination question in a set time—say ten or fifteen minutes. The different planning approaches could then be compared and discussed.

TOO MUCH REVISION?

It is difficult to imagine anyone doing too much revision for an examination, but revision done at the wrong time can be harmful.

(a) Do not revise when you are tired, because it is easy to become confused.

(b) Do not revise directly before going to bed, since, if your mind is very active at that point, you will not sleep properly.

(c) Do not revise the night before an examination. The process of revision coupled with pre-examination nerves can also make you confused. Planned revision will ensure that you are confident enough not to have to 'panic' revise.

F. CHECKLIST ✓ ✓ ✓ ✓ ✓ ✓ ✓ ✓ ✓ ✓ ✓

1	Revision should be part of a continuous programme.
2	Revision involves you in an active task.
3	You should continually revise your notes to fill in any gaps and to clarify and explain difficult concepts or theories.
4	Active revision will aid recall.
5	A card index can be very useful for revision notes and cross-referencing.
6	Experiment with different revision techniques to see which suits you best in particular circumstances.
7	Remember information by dividing your work into headings and subheadings.
8	Beware of using old essays for revision.
9	Revise in an appropriate environment. Be active, and remember that there are no short cuts!

A Revision Syndicate

THE EXAMINATION

Page

A. BEFORE THE EXAMINATION 158

B. THE RUBRIC 159

C. APPROACHING THE PAPER 159
    Reading through the Paper 160
    Selecting the Questions 160
    General Points about Writing 161
    Diagrams and Charts 161
    Looking at Statistics for the First Time 161

D. PLANNING YOUR ANSWER 163

E. WRITING YOUR ANSWER 165

F. A NOTE ABOUT TACKLING MULTIPLE-CHOICE QUESTIONS .. 165

G. CHECKLIST 166

A. BEFORE THE EXAMINATION

If your revision has been properly planned and you have kept to your plan, by the time the examination arrives you should be capable of performing well. No one can expect you to do more than your best. You should enter the examination prepared to do just this.

Directly before the examination, bear the following points in mind:

(a) Do not discuss last-minute points with other people. Trust your own revision and your own ability. Other people's ideas may lead you astray.

(b) Check that you have at least two pens as well as a pencil, pencil sharpener, rubber, ruler and, where allowed, a calculator. This may seem obvious, but every year people waste their own time and disturb others by having to ask for equipment.

(c) Try to keep as calm as possible before the examination, but do not worry if you feel a little nervous, as this can often help the adrenalin to flow.

B. THE RUBRIC

Well before the examination, your teacher should have explained just what will be required of you on each paper. Nevertheless, do not take the instructions on the front of the examination paper (the rubric) for granted. We all make mistakes. Study the rubric and make sure you understand it. Ask the examination invigilator for guidance if you are unsure about anything.

Some rubrics are straightforward, for example:

Answer three questions.

Other rubrics place limits on which questions you may answer, usually based on a sectionalised paper. For example:

Answer four questions, two from section A

and two from section B.

Do follow these instructions. If you do not obey the rubric, the offending answers will not be marked, and you will have wasted your time. Every year good candidates do badly in examinations by not following instructions properly.

C. APPROACHING THE PAPER

You should aim for the best possible performance in each paper you sit. The precise approach you take to each paper will depend on whether it contains multiple-choice questions, data-response questions or essays. Specific guidance on each of these is given in the relevant chapters. Nevertheless, there are some general principles to remember when approaching any examination paper.

(a) Where there is an element of choice involved in the paper, spend some time reading through the questions. Do not open the examination paper and start on the first question which you think you can do.

(b) Aim for an even performance throughout the paper. Remember that in order to achieve a good result, a good fourth question is as important as a good first question.

(c) Make good use of your time. Do not spend too long on one question if it means answering another one inadequately. If you only have time to answer three questions instead of four, you will have automatically lost 25% of your marks.

Reading Through the Paper

☐ You will need to read through an essay paper or a data-response paper slowly and carefully.

☐ Try to ignore the pressure created by the examination atmosphere.

☐ Be careful not to react to questions too quickly, since first impressions can be misleading.

☐ Work out exactly what each question is asking before considering whether or not you can answer it well.

☐ Having read the paper once, read it through a second time, marking the questions which you consider you can answer best. This may well take the first five or ten minutes of the examination. The rest of the time should be divided equally between each of the questions.

Selecting the Questions

Where you have a choice of questions, the selection of these will be crucial in determining your level of achievement. This requires time and thought.

(a) *Resist the temptation to begin writing straight away.* Spend time considering each question carefully.

(b) *Do not search the paper for familiar topics based on key words.* For example, just because you know something about inflation it does not mean that you will be able to answer *any* question on inflation. Use your skills of question analysis to decide whether or not to tackle a particular question.

(c) *Consider carefully what the question is about.* Again, do not rely on looking at key words. Make sure you understand exactly what the question expects you to do. Consider words like 'assess', 'appraise', 'discuss' and 'analyse'. The examiner will be looking at your ability to do what has been asked.

(d) *If a question has more than one part, consider whether you can indeed answer every part.* Make sure that you give each part its due. If weightings are given to each part, take this as an indication of how much the examiner expects you to write. Do not spend too long on a section worth only one mark, because generally the examiner will only be looking for one point. *Spend time in proportion to the marks awarded.* Where no weighting is given to parts of the question, assume that marks will be spread equally and divide up your time accordingly.

General Points about Writing

The content, clarity and line of argument of your answer will determine the mark range you receive. Details can add to your answer, but if they are irrelevant or inaccurate, they can detract from it. You should avoid writing everything you know about a subject when answering a question. This will only make the answer overrun. Moreover, if you adopt the 'write everything you know' strategy, you will not be directly answering the question as set and will not gain high marks.

Time is obviously a constraint. You should therefore cut out activities which are unnecessary. For example:

☐ Do not write out the question.

☐ Do not use liquid paper. You can often forget to write over it at a later stage. Put a line through an error.

☐ If you wish to insert material which you left out, do not squeeze it in. Use an asterisk at the appropriate point to indicate to the examiner that there is an extra sentence or paragraph to be read.

☐ Do not waste time with elaborate handwriting. Write as fast as you can without letting your writing become illegible.

> Candidates' scripts must be readable with normal effort on the part of the examiner. If this is not the case, full benefit for technical content may not be received, simply because the reader is partly guessing what the writer intended.
> University of London Examiners' Report:
> A Level Economics, June, 1984.

Diagrams and Charts

Use of diagrams and charts, as we have already seen, can be very useful in Economics. Often a diagram can convey much more than paragraphs of writing. But, as with everything in the examination situation, you are faced with a time constraint. Therefore remember the following principles:

● Only use a diagram when it adds something to your answer.

● Make sure the diagram is large, clear and clearly labelled. A diagram which leaves the examiner puzzled will be a waste of effort.

● In the text, fully explain the diagram and its implications.

● Do not make the diagram too intricate. It should be clear and to the point. Only add details which are strictly necessary. You will not gain marks for a diagram which looks like a work of art. You will be wasting your time.

> Candidates should decide whether a diagram is an effective way of illustrating or explaining the point to be made. If it is to be included then the time devoted to it should be in proportion to the importance of the point for the answer as a whole.
>
> Weaker candidates frequently draw inaccurate diagrams without comment, apparently assuming these to be self-explanatory. Candidates should use a ruler and a pencil for all diagrams and erase any errors.
> University of London Examiners' Report:
> A Level Economics, June, 1984.

Looking at Statistics for the First Time

In many questions, particularly data-response questions, you may be presented with a table of statistics. Because it can be very time-consuming to examine these in detail the first time you look through the paper, the following is a good strategy to adopt:

(a) Briefly look at the title of the table of statistics, the column headings and the row headings. These will tell you what the statistics cover.

(b) Look at the question or questions which follow the table and think about whether this is an area which you might be able to tackle. If it is one you are unfamiliar with, go on to the next question.

(c) If it is an area you think you could tackle, look again at the table of statistics and, by *scanning* the figures, try to get a feel for trends and relationships.

(d) Do not at this stage try to look at the statistics in detail. Leave that until you finally decide whether or not to tackle the question.

EXAMPLE

Look at the following macro-economic statistics which show the state of an imaginary economy between 1972 and 1987.

Notes:

1. In columns 1 to 4 the figures give the percentage change on the previous year.

2. In column 5 the figures relate to a given year.

Year	Column No. 1 % change in retail prices	2 % change in average weekly earnings	3 % change in import prices	4 % change in money stock (£M3)	5 Unemployment (%)
1972	7	12	5	27	3.5
1973	9	13	30	27	2.4
1974	16	19	55	11	2.9
1975	28	29	14	9	3.7
1976	19	16	22	10	5.0
1977	16	9	16	12	5.3
1978	8	13	4	16	5.4
1979	13	15	7	18	5.5
1980	20	21	10	19	6.1
1981	12	13	8	14	9.5
1982	9	9	8	11	10.0
1983	5	5	7	11	12.1
1984	4	4	9	10	12.6
1985	6	9	4	12	13.1
1986	5	8	6	11	13.2
1987	5	7	7	9	13.2

Question: *With reference to the statistics, examine the factors which have influenced retail prices.*

Your strategy

(i) Note that you are given data on five key macro-economic indicators between 1972 and 1987.

(ii) The question requires you to look at the relationship between the percentage change in the retail price index and the other indicators.

(iii) Look briefly at the statistics. You might note the following:
—very high inflation in 1975
—very high increases in earnings in the same year
—a large increase in import prices in 1974, probably caused by the oil price rise
—a steady increase in unemployment.
You will not have the time to spot much more.

(iv) Go on to the next question.

D. PLANNING YOUR ANSWER

A long essay is not necessarily a good essay. An essay of moderate length which is well structured and well argued is more likely to get good marks than one which rambles on, noting points as they arise in the student's mind. Quantity of material is less important than clarity of thought. A good essay will therefore only be produced if you spend a few minutes thinking about the way the essay should develop.

If you have forgotten the main principles behind planning an essay, look back at the chapter on essay-writing. Remember, though, that in the examination you are under a considerable time constraint, so your plans cannot be as elaborate as they would be under other circumstances.

> In many instances candidates are failing to realise their academic potential because of badly-structured answers and ignorance of how to present an argument. Candidates should be educated to plan their answers before commencement.
> University of London Examiners' Report: A Level Economics, June, 1984.

EXAMPLE

Consider the following essay question:

> *'The role of the government is towards the maintenance of a stable macro-economy. The free market should be left to deal with all other aspects.' To what extent is this a sensible approach for government policy-makers?*

If faced with that type of question in the examination, you need a sensible essay plan which will be simple to construct. The essay should be seen in two parts:
 (i) The role of the government in the macro-economy
 (ii) The role of the free market, the limitations of the free market, and the need for additional government intervention.

A sensible essay plan may therefore look something like the one on the next page.

This is less of a formal plan and more of a reminder about the key points which need to be included.

Advantages of this sort of plan:
☐ It provides a basic structure for the answer.
☐ Key points can be seen; these form the basis for paragraphs and sections in the answer. Details and reminders about examples can be included or added, but should not be allowed to overwhelm the plan itself.
☐ The plan acts as a memory aid. During its construction, you will be able to think of many of the details which will form the bulk of the essay.
☐ The plan prevents you from drying up. It facilitates a fast flow of writing without wasteful pauses. Points to be covered can be adjusted to time available.
☐ The plan is spaced out so as to leave room for points which are remembered during the writing of the essay but cannot be included in the essay at the stage they are actually remembered.
☐ By the time you have considered a plan, you will be better prepared to write a good introduction.

fiscal Policy
Monetary Policy
Stabilization Policy
↑
Income Redistribution
Balance of Payments
Reasonable growth
Low unemployment
Low inflation
↑
Macroeconomic policy
↑

Government Policy — vs. — free market

Disadvantages
(e.g more money = more power)
↑
Equilibrium determined by interaction of Supply and Demand
↑
Economic System
↑

Need for other types of policy because of
(microeconomic policy).

→ Market failure
↓
Public goods
(defence, street lights etc.)
Externalities
(pollution)
Social Welfare
(disadvantaged etc.)
Economic restructuring
(e.g retraining structurally unemployed)

EXERCISE

Draw up examination essay plans for the following essay titles. You should not spend any longer than five minutes on each one:

(i) *Discuss how you would set about assessing the benefits of multinational corporations to host nations' economies. Do you consider that there will be costs involved as well?*

(ii) *Explain the difference between proportional, progressive and regressive taxes. With reference to the U.K. economy, give examples of each type of tax.*

(iii)

Marketable wealth in the U.K. (%)				
Percentage of wealth owned by:	*1971*	*1976*	*1979*	*1982*
Most wealthy 1% of population	31	24	22	21
Most wealthy 5% of population	52	43	40	41
Most wealthy 10% of population	65	57	54	56
Most wealthy 50% of population	97	95	95	96

Source: Social Trends, HMSO, 1985.

Identify the changing distribution of wealth in the United Kingdom between 1971 and 1982. Discuss the factors which could have caused these changes.

E. WRITING YOUR ANSWER

Most of the advice needed to enable you to write a good essay or data-response answer is contained in earlier chapters of this book. The quality of your answer will depend on the depth of your knowledge and the skills you have acquired over your period of study.

A few specific pieces of guidance can be added at this final stage:

(a) The length of your answer should be appropriate to the examination situation. The luxury of a long complex essay will not be given to you in an examination. Spend an appropriate amount of time on each question.

(b) Never assume that the examiner will fill in details for you. Write as if you were explaining something to an intelligent but uninformed reader. Be particularly careful about using economic terms without making clear what they mean.

(c) Be careful about the logical development of your essay. Do not jump about from point to point. Use paragraphs to separate different ideas clearly. In each case, link the paragraph to the one that has gone before and to the question title. Explain new themes and use examples where possible.

(d) Make your writing explicit, relevant and to the point. Straying off the subject will not gain you marks and will cost you time. At intervals, glance back at the question to make sure you are still answering it in a relevant way.

> A soundly-structured answer opens by outlining how the question is to be approached and makes clear any assumptions that are made. The main part should deal systematically with the relevant points with each point treated in a separate paragraph.
> University of London Examiners' Report:
> A Level Economics, June, 1984.

F. A NOTE ABOUT TACKLING MULTIPLE-CHOICE QUESTIONS

Most of the advice given in this chapter relates directly to writing examination answers based on essay or data-response questions. Remember that you will often be required to sit a series of multiple-choice questions as well. Below are some specific guidelines about answering these in the examination situation:

(a) *Plan your time properly.* If there are fifty questions to be answered in two hours, allow approximately two minutes per question.

(b) *If a question proves difficult for you, leave it and return to it later.* Do not spend time struggling over one question, which could lead to your having no time to answer ones you could have done.

(c) *Generally, there is no need to read the paper through first since you will be tackling every question.* But check that you know exactly how many questions there are to be answered.

(d) *Do not make wild guesses at answers.* Even if you are not sure of an answer, you should be able to eliminate certain possibilities. At the very least you can then allow yourself an informed guess.

(e) *Answer every question.*

G. CHECKLIST ✓ ✓ ✓ ✓ ✓ ✓ ✓ ✓ ✓ ✓ ✓

1	Be well prepared.
2	Make sure well in advance that you are aware of the structure of each paper you sit.
3	Check the rubric.
4	When you open your paper, do not panic. The approach you take should have been prepared in advance. Where appropriate, read the paper carefully. Stick to a time plan.
5	Plan essay questions carefully.
6	Bear the question in mind at all times.
7	Keep your eye on the clock.